REFORMATION, EXPLORATION, AND EMPIRE

Volume 5

IRELAND–MANUFACTURING

an imprint of

■SCHOLASTIC

www.scholastic.com/librarypublishing

Published by Grolier,
an imprint of Scholastic Library Publishing,
Sherman Turnpike
Danbury, Connecticut 06816

© 2005 The Brown Reference Group plc

Set ISBN 0-7172-6071-2
Volume 5 ISBN 0-7172-6076-3

Library of Congress Cataloging-in-Publication Data

Reformation, exploration, and empire.
    p. cm.
    Contents: Vol. 1. Academies–Catherine de Médicis —
v. 2. Catholic church–daily life — v. 3. Decorative arts–
fortifications — v. 4. France–inventions and inventors —
v. 5. Ireland–manufacturing — v. 6. Maps and
mapmaking–Orthodox church — v. 7. Ottoman Empire–
printing — v. 8. Privacy and luxury–sculpture — v. 9.
Servants–textiles — v. 10. Thirteen Colonies–Zwingli.
    Includes bibliographical references and index.
    ISBN 0-7172-6071-2 (set : alk. paper) — ISBN 0-7172-
6072-0 (v. 1 : alk. paper) — ISBN 0-7172-6073-9 (v. 2 :
alk. paper) — ISBN 0-7172-6074-7 (v. 3 : alk. paper) —
ISBN 0-7172-6075-5 (v. 4 : alk. paper) — ISBN 0-7172-
6076-3 (v. 5 : alk. paper) — ISBN 0-7172-6077-1 (v. 6 :
alk. paper) — ISBN 0-7172-6078-X (v. 7 : alk. paper) —
ISBN 0-7172-6079-8 (v. 8 : alk.paper) — ISBN 0-7172-
6080-1 (v. 9 : alk. paper) — ISBN 0-7172-6081-X (v. 10 :
alk. paper)
    1. History, Modern—16th century—Encyclopedias,
Juvenile. 2. History, Modern—17th century—
Encyclopedias, Juvenile. 3 Renaissance—Encyclopedias,
Juvenile. 4 Civilization, Modern—17th century—
Encyclopedias, Juvenile. 5 Reformation—Encyclopedias,
Juvenile. I. Grolier (Firm)

D228.R46 2005
909'.5'03—dc22   2004063255

For information address the publisher:
Grolier, Sherman Turnpike,
Danbury, Connecticut 06816

FOR THE BROWN REFERENCE GROUP

Project Editor: Emily Hill
Deputy Editor: Tom Webber
Text Editor: Rachel Bean
Picture Researcher: Susy Forbes
Maps: Darren Awuah
Design Manager: Lynne Ross
Design: Q2A Solutions
Production Director: Alastair Gourlay
Editorial Director: Lindsey Lowe
Senior Managing Editor: Tim Cooke
Consultant: Prof. James M. Murray
                           University of Cincinnati

Printed and bound in Singapore

ABOUT THIS SET

This is one of a set of 10 books about the key period of western history from around 1500 to around 1700. The defining event of the age was the Reformation, the attempt to reform the Catholic church that resulted in a permanent split in western Christianity. The period was also marked by the European exploration and colonization of new lands, profound political change, and dynamic cultural achievement.

The roots of the Reformation lay in a tradition of protest against worldliness and corruption in the Catholic church. In 1517 the German Augustinian monk Martin Luther produced a list of criticisms of Catholicism and sparked a protest movement that came to be known as Protestantism. The reformers broke away from Catholicism and established new Protestant churches. In response the Catholic church launched the Counter Reformation, its own program of internal reforms.

Religious change had a profound political influence as Protestantism was adopted by various rulers to whom it offered a useful way to undermine Europe's existing power structures. The period was one of intolerance, persecution, and almost continuous warfare. Meanwhile new approaches to religion combined with the spread of printing and increased literacy to produce a knowledge revolution in which new ideas flourished about science, art, and humanity's place in the universe.

Changes in Europe had a lasting effect on events elsewhere. Spanish conquistadors overthrew vast empires in the Americas, while Catholic missionaries spread Christianity in Africa, the Americas, and Asia. Gradually lands in the east and the west were penetrated and colonized by Europeans. These and other important changes, such as the development of international trade, great cultural achievements, and the spirit of learning, are explored in detail in each volume.

While focusing mainly on Europe, the set also looks at important developments across Africa, Asia, and the Americas. Each entry ends with a list of cross references to related entries so that you can follow up particular topics. Contemporary illustrations give a fuller picture of life during the Reformation. Each volume contains a glossary, a "Further Reading" list that includes websites, a timeline, and an index covering the whole set.

Contents

Volume 5

IRELAND

Between 1500 and 1700 English control gradually replaced the power of ruling Irish families in Ireland. Irish landowners, who were mainly Catholic, had their land confiscated, and English monarchs invited Protestant settlers to colonize the country.

In 1500 the monarch of England was also the ruler of Ireland. However, there was little English involvement in Irish matters. Different regions of Ireland were ruled by different lords of Gaelic (native Irish) or Anglo-Norman descent. The Fitzgerald family, which ruled Kildare in eastern Ireland, had established itself as the foremost lordship. The English kings Henry VII (ruled 1485–1509) and Henry VIII (ruled 1509–1547) recognized the power of the Fitzgerald family by appointing successive earls of Kildare as lord-lieutenant, their representative in Ireland.

CHALLENGING AUTHORITY

In 1534 Thomas, Lord Offaly, the 10th earl of Kildare, heard rumors that his father, who had been imprisoned in the Tower of London for failing as lord-lieutenant, had been executed (his father actually died of natural causes the following year). In protest Thomas led an uprising. A devoted Catholic, Thomas also branded Henry VIII a heretic because the king had just split England from the authority of Rome. Henry responded by suppressing the rebellion, confiscating all the Fitzgerald lands, and executing most of the family.

Gaelic lords in the Irish midlands took advantage of the Fitzgeralds' demise by claiming new territories. To restore control, Henry set about removing the lords from their lands. Only those who promised to recognize the English king as their ruler, lay down their arms, and introduce English laws and customs were exempted.

After the Fitzgerald uprising the post of lord-lieutenant passed to English Protestants. One famous lord-lieutenant was Henry Sidney (served 1565–1579), who gave land to English merchants and adventurers in the hope that they would bring English families to settle on their estates.

In this illustration Lord Thomas Fitzgerald, 10th earl of Kildare, throws down his sword at Saint Mary's Abbey, Dublin, in 1534. After hearing wrongly that Henry VIII had executed his father, Thomas renounced his allegiance to the king.

Sidney's scheme heightened tensions in Ireland and led to further uprisings against English rule in Ireland. In 1579 the Desmond family rebelled, but Elizabeth I (ruled 1558–1603) suppressed the revolt.

In the 1590s Hugh O'Neill, the earl of Tyrone, raised a rebel army. His victories sparked a general revolt. Other nobles supported him, as did King Philip II of Spain, who supplied O'Neill with 4,000 soldiers. O'Neill's army was so large that Elizabeth sent 20,000 soldiers to Ireland. In 1601 they defeated O'Neill's forces at the Battle of Kinsale. The uprising finally ended in 1603, marking the end of Irish control of the country.

PLANTATION OF ULSTER

James I (ruled 1603–1625) introduced a colonization drive that, between 1603 and 1641, led to the settlement of around 100,000 English and Scottish people in Ireland. Many towns were established, including Londonderry, so-called because London companies sent men and money to rebuild the medieval town of Derry in 1613. James required all Irish landowners to become Protestant, but missionaries from continental Europe were already at work strengthening Catholicism.

In 1641 an Irish rebellion led to the deaths of up to 2,000 settlers. The English Civil War of the 1640s prevented an immediate response to the rebellion; but when Oliver Cromwell became head of the English government in 1649, he began a bloody campaign to impose English rule in Ireland, suppressing uprisings in the cities of Drogheda and Wexford with great savagery. Cromwell introduced a transplantation policy, removing Irish landowners to the western province of Connacht and granting lands in the rest of Ireland to English soldiers.

Thousands of Irish people were also shipped to the West Indies to work as indentured laborers to make way for English settlers.

PROTESTANT CONTROL

After the restoration of the English monarchy in 1660 Ireland experienced a period of peace. Catholics were tolerated, and the economy grew. The unpopular transplantation policy was in place until 1685, when the Catholic King James II came to the throne. His efforts to restore land to Catholics alarmed English and Irish Protestants.

In the Glorious Revolution of 1688 the Dutch Protestant William of Orange and his wife Mary replaced James as rulers. James fled to France, then went to Ireland in an attempt to regain his throne. The Irish Parliament in Dublin recognized him as king, but William defeated James at the Battle of the Boyne in 1690 forcing James into permanent exile. Successive English monarchs continued to rule Ireland as a kingdom separate from England.

This illustration from 1649 shows Oliver Cromwell attacking the Irish city of Drogheda. Cromwell restored English control following a number of revolts in Ireland. His brutal suppression of the Irish is still remembered.

SEE ALSO

- Catholic church
- Counter Reformation
- Elizabeth I
- English Commonwealth
- Glorious Revolution
- William of Orange

ISLAM

The 16th and 17th centuries was a period when Islamic states ruled West and Central Asia, India, North Africa, and southeastern Europe. Three great Islamic empires emerged: the Turkish Ottoman Empire, the Safavid Empire in Persia, and the Mogul Empire in India.

The reasons for Islam's spread are complex and involved politics, military power, and the nature of Islam itself. Islam was founded in the seventh century, when the Prophet Muhammad received the revelations that would form the Muslim holy book, the Koran. Despite the early persecution of Muhammad's followers, their numbers grew rapidly.

When Muhammad died in 632, he left a Muslim state of 100,000 people centered on the cities of Medina and Mecca in present-day Saudi Arabia. The state was organized under successive rulers called caliphs. To expand their territory and make converts, the caliphs began a series of military conquests. Over the next century Muslim armies advanced across North Africa, Spain, and southern France, and to the east across Central Asia into Pakistan.

There were three powerful Muslim empires in the 16th and 17th centuries. The first to emerge was the Ottoman Empire, which from small beginnings

Muslim pilgrims crowd into the Great Mosque in Mecca, Saudi Arabia, Islam's holiest city and center of the first Muslim empire in the seventh century.

ISLAMIC ARTS

Religious traditions strongly influenced Islamic arts. The aim of Muslim artists and craftsmen was to glorify God. Since the Koran contains the word of God, Muslims considered calligraphy, or decorative lettering, to be the highest art form. Decorative Arabic script was incorporated into art forms, such as metalwork, ceramics, textiles, and in architectural details on buildings. According to religious tradition only the most devout Muslims could practice calligraphy.

In addition to calligraphy geometric patterns were an important part of Islamic design. Complex geometric patterns were used to symbolize the order of the created universe. Often designs had one small error in them to emphasize that only God is a perfect creator. Both these design elements were used in a number of different art forms.

Islam did not specifically forbid pictoral art, but it was discouraged. Figurative art in the Islamic world is generally nonreligious. In the 16th century there was a flowering of miniature painting in the Safavid Empire in Persia (modern Iran). Miniature painting was later imported into India by the Mogul Emperor, Akbar the Great.

in Anatolia (in what is now Turkey) in around 1300 eventually rose to conquer the Balkans, Syria, western Arabia, and much of North Africa. In 1453 the Ottomans took the city of Constantinople (now Istanbul) the center of eastern Christianity. Then they launched campaigns in Europe. Suleyman the Magnificent (ruled 1520–1566) gained control of most of Hungary in 1526, and pushed into Austria to besiege Vienna in 1529.

SAFAVIDS AND MOGULS

The second major Islamic empire was the Safavid Empire in Persia (now Iran). Unlike the Ottoman Empire that was made up of Sunni Muslims, the Safavid Empire was made up of Shia Muslims (*see box p. 8*). The Safavid Dynasty was founded by Shah Esmail in 1501. It spread across West Asia to Afghanistan in the east and Iraq in the west, reaching its greatest extent under Abbas I (ruled 1588–1629).

The third major Islamic empire was that of the Moguls in India, which also arose in the 16th century. The empire was founded in 1526 by the warrior Babur, who was of Mongol descent and ruled over a kingdom in Afghanistan when he first invaded India in 1519.

Babur occupied only the northernmost territories of India, but later Mogul rulers extended the borders of the empire to include almost the entire Indian subcontinent by 1707.

PEACE AND WAR

Islam was the main religion across large areas of Europe, Asia, and North Africa by the 17th century. However,

The Mogul emperor of India, Jahangir (ruled 1605–1627), embraces Abbas I, the Safavid shah of Persia (ruled 1588–1629), in 1620. Jahangir had a Persian wife, Nur Jahan, whose relatives played a major role in the politics of Mogul India.

SUNNI AND SHIA ISLAM

The division of Islam into Sunni and Shia branches occurred after the death of the Prophet Muhammad in 632. The young Islamic state that Muhammad had founded had to find itself a leader and spiritual successor. One group of Muslims elected a leader—Abu Bakr—known as a caliph, while a smaller group argued that the caliph should come from Muhammad's family itself, in the first instance his son-in-law, Ali. The Muslims who believed in the elected caliphate were known as Sunni Muslims, while those who believed in family succession were the Shia Muslims.

These divisions exist today, despite the fact that the Sunnis abolished the caliphate in 1924, believing that the force of Islamic law is enough to unify the Islamic world. Sunnis are still the majority branch of Islam. Sunni Islam places emphasis on social order and the law, based on the views and customs of the majority of the community.

In contrast, Shia Muslims hold that an imam, a natural successor of Muhammad, can reveal God's truth in much the same way as the pope is believed to be the final authority in Catholicism. In the absence of an imam authorities known as mujtahidun or (in Iran) ayatollahs govern the interpretation of the law. ("Imam" is also the term used for a person who leads prayers in a mosque.) Shia Islam also focuses more on the mystical inner life of the individual.

the Islamic empires were not unified by faith. There were two main branches of Islam: Sunni and Shia. Sunni Islam was practiced by the Ottomans, and Shia Islam by the Safavids. The theological differences between the Sunnis and Shiites contributed to the wars between the Ottomans and Safavids from 1578 to 1590 and from 1603 to 1619. At the same time, the Ottomans were fighting with Europeans. During the Ottoman conflict with the Hapsburgs from 1593 to 1606 the Safavids supported the military operations of the Hapsburgs.

For the Ottomans, fighting wars on two fronts was a huge burden. Cyprus

This copy of the Koran, the holy book of Islam, was created during the reign of Ottoman Sultan Bayezid the Just (ruled 1481–1512). Bayezid is famous for the support he gave to the development of culture in the Ottoman Empire.

was added to the empire in 1571 and Tunis in 1574, but the Ottomans also suffered a heavy defeat at Lepanto in 1571, where almost their entire navy was destroyed. They recovered to resume their policy of territorial expansion. However, with the defeat of their last great expedition against Vienna in 1683 the Ottomans entered a long period of decline.

Likewise, the Safavid Empire also began to decline in the 17th century, despite reaching a peace settlement with the Ottomans in 1639 (the Peace of Zuhab) that established the border between the two empires—the present-day border between Iran and Iraq. The Safavid Empire effectively collapsed in 1736 following the invasion of its territory by Afghan warrior tribes in 1722. In India the Mogul Empire reached its greatest extent in 1707, but thereafter it too shrank dramatically, so that only the extreme north remained in Mogul hands by 1765.

TRANSFORMING THE WORLD

Although all three major Islamic empires would decline, the dynamic spread of Islam changed the nature of the world forever. Islamic trade routes now crossed lands stretching from the Balkans in Europe to the borders of India. Along them moved merchants—carrying cloth, rare jewels, precious metals, and spices—and huge numbers of Muslims taking part in the *hajj* (the pilgrimage to Mecca every Muslim is required to make at least once in their life if they have the means). Such travelers aided the spread of Islamic faith, culture, and art (*see box p. 7*).

The Islamic world had a huge influence on Europe, for example, in providing sources that inspired the scientific and technological advances of the 16th and 17th centuries. Europeans too had a great effect on the Islamic

world. From around 1498—when the Portuguese explorer Vasco da Gama rounded the Cape of Good Hope and sailed across the Indian Ocean to the west coast of India—first Portugal and then the Netherlands, England, and France steadily created trading outposts and colonies along coasts from Africa to China. As they did so, they took more and more territory from the Muslims and others, and threatened to take over control of trade between Europe and Asia. The Muslims were increasingly forced to rely on overland routes as Europeans began to assert their rule over maritime trade across the Indian Ocean.

Ceramic tiles depict the Great Mosque in Mecca with the Kaaba—the most holy shrine of Islam—at its center.

SEE ALSO

- Africa
- Akbar
- India
- Ottoman Empire
- Persia
- Suleyman the Magnificent

ISTANBUL

Istanbul lies on the crossroads between the Muslim world in Asia and the centers of Christianity in Europe. As the capital of the Turkish Ottoman Empire from the mid-15th century, Istanbul became one of the most sophisticated and affluent cities in the world.

Istanbul sits on a peninsula between Europe and Asia, in between the Aegean and Black seas. The city had two previous identities. In the eighth century B.C. Greek settlers founded a settlement on the site of the city in what is today northwest Turkey. This colony grew into a city named Byzantium, which eventually fell under Roman control. In 324 A.D. Roman Emperor Constantine declared Byzantium the capital of the empire, renaming it Constantinople. It remained the capital of the eastern Roman Empire, later the Byzantine Empire, until the 15th century.

THE OTTOMAN TAKEOVER
In 1422 Murad II, the Ottoman sultan, laid siege to Constantinople. He failed to take the city, but 30 years later in 1453 his son, Mehmed II (1432–1481), succeeded. The Ottomans blockaded supplies to the city from across the Black Sea and the Bosporus, and used powerful siege cannons to destroy its defenses. They occupied the city, massacring the civilians and plundering what was left of the city's riches. The Turks called the city Istanbul.

When Mehmed II took control of the city, his first act was to convert the cathedral of Hagia Sophia into a mosque. Although the city had been ravaged by centuries of conflict, Mehmed relocated the Ottoman capital from Edirne to Istanbul and began to

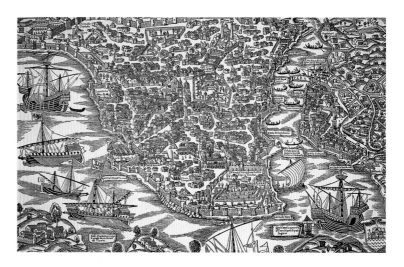

repopulate the city, bringing in new inhabitants from territories conquered by the Ottomans, particularly the Balkans. Mehmed also started transforming many of Istanbul's churches into mosques, establishing the city as a major center of the Islamic world. However, Mehmed demonstrated his tolerance of other religions by preserving the Orthodox church and allowing it to appoint a new patriarch, or head. Mehmed also ordered the construction of imperial palaces in the city, the most striking of which, Topkapi Palace, still stands. In 1477 Istanbul had a population of around 70,000; by 1580 the population stood at 500,000.

LIFE IN OTTOMAN ISTANBUL
Although the Ottoman Turks were Muslims, only about 60 percent of Istanbul's population was Islamic.

This map of Istanbul dates from 1520. In that year Suleyman the Magnificent became sultan of the Ottoman Empire. Suleyman encouraged art and culture centered on the city during a period that is considered to be a golden age.

The rest were Christians or Jews. Non-Muslims were free to practice their religion as long as they paid a special tax. Non-Muslims held some of the most prestigious jobs. Most court physicians, for example, were Jewish.

Although Europeans considered the Ottomans to be a major threat to Christian Europe, they were fascinated by the city of Istanbul. One 16th-century European traveler, Pierre Gilles, a French botanist sent by King Francis I of France, said of Istanbul, "Earth's cities are doomed to perish sooner or later, but as long as mankind remains on earth, this city will endure."

A modern view of the Suleymaniye Mosque in Istanbul, built in 1555. Designed by the leading architect Sinan, the mosque is the grandest example of Ottoman architecture in Istanbul.

EXPANSION

Istanbul thrived under Ottoman rule, particularly during the reign of Suleyman the Magnificent (ruled 1520–1566). He transformed the city, building a new water supply, fountains, and public baths. He built numerous mosques, palaces, and decorative sculptures. One of the finest architects in Istanbul was Sinan (1490–1580). He designed more than 350 buildings in the city, including the Seyzade Mosque (1548) and the Suleymaniye Mosque (1555), which he modeled on the city's magnificent former cathedral, Hagia Sofia. In the early 1600s Sultan Ahmed I commissioned the architect Mehmed Aga to build the Blue Mosque. It was shrouded in controversy because it had six minarets (slender towers from which Muslims are called to prayer), and only the Great Mosque in Mecca had as many. Since Mecca was the most holy place in the Islamic world, some Muslims felt it was sacrilegious to compete with the Great Mosque.

From 1700 Istanbul continued to be a center of Islam, trade, and commerce, providing Asia with an important link to Europe. Sustained contact with Europeans, however, led Istanbul to become increasingly westernized.

ISTANBUL'S EARTHQUAKES

The biggest threat to daily life in Ottoman Istanbul came not from war but from nature. Earthquakes are common in the region. Located on the North Anatolian fault, a 560-mile (900-km) crack between earth's tectonic plates, Istanbul is in constant danger from tremors and major earthquakes. The first recorded earthquake in Istanbul during the Ottoman period was in 1489. A more powerful one occurred in 1509, which was referred to in contemporary accounts as "The Lesser Judgment Day," destroying more than 100 mosques and 1,000 other buildings. Around 10,000 people died during this quake and its aftershocks. Between 1556 and 1754 eight further serious earthquakes were recorded. Even today modern Istanbul lives under the threat of earthquakes.

SEE ALSO

• Islam
• Jews and Judaism
• Orthodox church
• Ottoman Empire
• Suleyman the Magnificent

ITALIAN STATES

During the early decades of the 16th century the Italian states were convulsed by wars in which France and Spain struggled to gain domination. Spain was victorious and controlled the fortunes of the Italian states to varying degrees until the 18th century.

During the 16th and 17th centuries, as for much of its history, the Italian Peninsula was not a unified political region but a collection of independent states. These states varied in size, composition, and political structure, and had long vied with each other to dominate the power balance in the region. In the late 15th century and the first half of the 16th century the powerful nations of France and Spain turned their attentions to Italy, invading the peninsula and seeking to extend their rule there.

PROSPERING CITY-STATES

The city-states of northern and central Italy had become wealthy in the 14th and 15th centuries as centers of trade, the production of luxury goods, and banking. As they prospered, they incorporated more territories around their urban centers. These flourishing city-states included republics with elected governments, such as Venice and Genoa in the north and Florence in central Italy. They also included duchies under the control of powerful aristocratic families, such as the duchy of Milan in the north. As time went on, many republics also came to be dominated by a few powerful families.

During the 15th century the prosperity, relative stability, and civic pride of many of these city-states provided a fertile setting for the revival of classical (ancient Greek and Roman)

learning and the flowering of the arts known as the Renaissance. Florence in particular became a great center of the arts in the 15th century.

Venice had grown hugely rich on its sea trade, particularly its monopoly of the import of spices from Asia. From the 15th century the Venetians consolidated their commercial success

This painting, made in about 1600, shows an aerial view of Venice. The city was at the heart of one of the strongest Italian states of the 16th century.

by acquiring territories and cities on the Italian mainland; Venice itself was built on a series of islands in a lagoon. By the beginning of the 16th century many Italian states felt threatened by Venice's prosperity and growth.

PAPAL STATES AND THE SOUTH

In central Italy the pope, who was a territorial ruler as well as the spiritual leader of the Catholic church, ruled extensive lands known as the Papal States. From the mid-15th century successive popes made the Papal States a major power in central Italy. Pope Julius II (pope 1503–1513) is notable for the effort he made to consolidate the position of the Papal States. He also patronized religious art projects in Rome, making it a center of the Catholic church. From 1600 the power of the Papal States began to wane. However, Rome continued to be a major center of artistic patronage.

The Kingdom of Naples covered the southern part of the Italian Peninsula and was closely linked to the Kingdom of Sicily. Since the 13th century French Angevin monarchs had ruled Naples, and Spanish Aragonese kings and queens had controlled Sicily. In 1442 Naples fell to the Aragonese King Alfonso V of Sicily, who became king of both states.

FRAGMENTATION AND WAR

In some respects the existence of many separate Italian states had been an impetus for the Renaissance, the rivalries between different cities spurring them to invest in ever more ambitious buildings and works of art. In other ways, however, it was destructive: The history of the Italian states is one of almost constant unrest, territorial acquisition and loss, shifting alliances, and war. When France and Spain fought over the region, they were

able to exploit existing divisions between the Italian states.

The Italian Wars began in 1494 when the French King Charles VIII (ruled 1483–1498) invaded Italy to seize the Spanish Kingdom of Naples. Milan and other states allowed Charles's troops to march through their territory because they wanted French help with their own plans. The struggle for Naples continued until 1504, when Spain finally won it back. Milan later became one of the most fought over territories of the wars, because of its tactically important location on routes between Italy and the rest of Europe.

The foreign invasions caused political upheaval in central Italy. The Medici, the ruling family of Florence, had declared loyalty to Spain and were ousted when the French invaded.

This map shows the main Italian states at the beginning of the 16th century.

THE KINGDOM OF NAPLES

The Kingdom of Naples became a center of power and culture in Europe in the 13th century. Under Aragonese kings in the 1400s the kingdom experienced economic and cultural growth. It was enriched particularly by artisans and merchants fleeing the 1453 Ottoman invasion of Constantinople. When Spain secured control of Naples in 1504, the kingdom became the main center of Spanish rule in Italy for the course of the Italian Wars. The Spanish monarchy asserted control through a viceroy, a chief officer who presided over the kingdom's most important ruling body, the Collateral Council. Viceroys such as Pedro de Toledo (served 1532–1553) worked to curb the power of local barons and improve the city of Naples. However, they also imposed heavy taxes on behalf of the Spanish king. In addition, the Spanish did little to address social inequalities that had long existed in the Kingdom of Naples. Provoked by high taxes, lower- and middle-class citizens rebelled in the Revolt of Masaniello (1647). The revolt was suppressed, but the kingdom continued its decline.

A fair fills the main square in Naples in this 17th-century picture.

Tuscan cities that the French had liberated from Florentine rule continued their revolt. Meanwhile, with French support the Florentine noble Cesare Borgia carved out a realm for himself from the Papal States.

To prevent the expansion of the powerful Venetian Republic, Italian and foreign powers joined together in the League of Cambrai (1508), which included the Holy Roman emperor, France, Spain, and Pope Julius II. The league won decisively at the Battle of Agnadello in 1509 but failed to take advantage due to the differing interests of its members. In 1510 the league collapsed when the pope switched sides and joined Venice. The pope then persuaded Spain to join him and Venice in an anti-French Holy League. This league drove the French from Milan but soon fell apart.

FRANCIS I AND CHARLES V

Local interests in Italy were subordinated to the dynastic rivalries of the new French and Spanish kings: Francis I (ruled 1515–1547) in France and Charles I (ruled 1516–1556) in Spain. (Charles was also elected Holy Roman emperor in 1519.)

Milan became a key battleground between 1515 and 1525. In 1525 Charles's army scored a crushing victory over France at the Battle of Pavia. However, Francis soon formed a new anti-Spanish alliance, the Holy League of Cognac, which included the pope, Milan, Florence, and Venice.

Partly to punish the pope for joining the Holy League but also because they had not been paid for several months, Charles's troops sacked Rome in May 1527, committing horrific atrocities. The pope was forced into hiding for months. News of the barbaric event shocked Europe, and the sack of Rome is sometimes considered to mark the end of the Renaissance in Italy. It was a devastating blow.

In 1529 Charles made peace with the pope in the Treaty of Barcelona and with Francis in the Treaty of Cambrai. Francis renounced his Italian claims; the last Sforza was allowed to rule Milan on condition that the duchy passed to Spain on his death, Venice lost its mainland conquests, and the Papal States were restored. The treaties brought to an end some 40 years of Spanish and French fighting in Italy. Although the French made several further military interventions in the region over the next decades, Spain had established its dominion in Italy.

SPANISH DOMINATION

Spain ruled several Italian states directly, while others retained their own rule but were answerable to, and often dependent on, their Spanish overlords. Naples, Sicily, Milan, and Sardinia were ruled directly through systems that combined weakened forms of their traditional governing bodies with chief officers and councils appointed by Spain (*see box opposite*). Their affairs were coordinated by the Council of Italy in the Spanish capital Madrid.

Elsewhere Italian states depended on Spanish backing. The Medici owed their restoration to power in Florence to Spain. The fortunes of Genoa were also closely linked to Spain. Its ships boosted the Spanish navy, and its banking families were powerful in Naples and Seville. In return, Spanish intervention helped avert civil war in the city in 1575. The papacy, too, was politically dependent on Spain. From the 1530s the popes expended most of their energies on the religious reforms of the Counter Reformation and the rebuilding of Rome. Only Venice was strong enough to keep its independence from Spain, although its trade was affected by Ottoman expansion in the eastern Mediterranean.

STABILITY AND DECLINE

Spanish domination brought peace and relative stability to Italy. In the second half of the 16th century many states prospered. Farming, the textile industry,

and banking flourished. However, the 17th century saw a decline in the wealth and cultural brilliance of most cities. In states directly ruled by Spain this decline was partly because of the heavy taxes imposed by the Spanish to help pay for costly wars elsewhere, as well as social inequality and unrest.

In some respects Italy's changing fortunes reflect a general lessening of Spain's dominance in the 1600s. They were also a result of broader economic trends. One of the most significant was the shift of trade away from the Mediterranean to the Atlantic. This transition occurred after the Portuguese discovery of sea routes to Asia and Spain's exploitation of its American territories. The death of the last Spanish Hapsburg king, Charles II, in 1700 brought to an end more than 150 years of Spanish domination in Italy.

Ships at anchor in Genoa's harbor in this late 16th-century painting are evidence of its naval power.

SEE ALSO

- Counter Reformation
- France
- Government, systems of
- Italian Wars
- Medici family
- Papacy
- Renaissance
- Rome
- Spain
- Venice

ITALIAN WARS

The Italian Wars from 1494 to 1559 were essentially a struggle between the Valois kings of France and the Hapsburg rulers of Spain for control of the independent states of Italy. They reflected the many changes in the nature of warfare that took place in the 15th and 16th centuries.

The Italian Wars began when Charles VIII, king of France (ruled 1483–1498), invaded Italy in 1494 to make a claim to rule of the southern Kingdom of Naples. The following year he briefly entered Naples but was forced to withdraw by a league of Italian states, the pope, and Spain. In 1504 Spanish forces captured Naples.

STRUGGLE FOR MILAN

In northern Italy Louis XII, the next king of France (ruled 1498–1515), asserted his claim to the wealthy duchy of Milan in 1499. This expansion of French territory alarmed Pope Julius II (pope 1503–1513), who organized a Holy League—made up of the Holy Roman Empire, Spain, England, and Venice—to drive the French out of Milan in 1512.

Prior to its foreign occupation, Milan was among the most successful examples of princely rule. It was restored in 1512 to Massimiliano (ruled 1512–1515), a member of the Sforza family, although the Swiss troops in control of Milan only allowed him symbolic rule. In 1515 Francis I, king of France (ruled 1515–1547), invaded Milan and defeated the Swiss, once more taking possession of the duchy.

When Holy Roman Emperor Maximilian I (ruled 1493–1519) died, his grandson, Charles, duke of Burgundy and king of Spain since 1516, was elected. He became known

as Charles V. Charles regarded the northern states of Milan and Genoa as important territories to control. Francis I was determined to hold onto his Italian territories. Thus the battle to control Milan continued.

In 1522 the French were forced to surrender military control of Milan, and in 1525 Francis I suffered a political and military setback when

Charles VIII of France enters Naples in 1495. He was soon forced to withdraw by an alliance that included Spain.

Charles defeated him at the Battle of Pavia. Francis's horse was shot dead under him, and the king was wounded and captured. He was kept prisoner in Spain until he agreed to give up French claims to Italian territory. Shortly after he was freed, Francis I went back on his agreement and, instead, struck an alliance with Pope Clement VII (pope 1523–1534) to form a new Holy League against Charles V. Charles's troops in Italy sacked Rome in 1527, partly in response to the formation of the Holy League but also out of desperation because they had not been paid for several months. Francis renounced his claim to territories in Italy in the Treaty of Cambrai, signed in 1529.

The Spaniards restored the Sforza hereditary claimant, Francesco II (ruled intermittently from 1521 to 1535), to nominal power in Milan. Francesco's death in 1535 was followed by direct rule by Spanish imperial governors, backed by occupying Spanish troops. There were further French offensives from 1536 to 1538 and from 1542 to 1544, but they achieved little.

TREATY OF CATEAU-CAMBRÉSIS

King Henry II (ruled 1547–1559) of France resumed war against Charles V in 1551. After defeating Charles in 1552, Henry took control of the archbishoprics of Metz, Verdun, and Toul in Lorraine, within the Holy Roman Empire. Further conflicts raged between Spanish and French forces.

In 1556 Charles V abdicated, handing over his western Hapsburg lands, including Spain, to his son Philip II (ruled 1556–1598). In 1559 Philip and Henry agreed to end the Italian Wars in the Treaty of Cateau-Cambrésis. The French gave up all their claims in Italy but kept their recently acquired territory in Lorraine.

KEY BATTLES

1494 King Charles VIII of France invades Italy and seizes Naples

1495 Battle of Fornovo; Charles's army loses to a combined force of King Ferdinand V of Spain, Holy Roman Emperor Maximilian I, Pope Alexander VI, and the republics of Venice and Milan

1499 King Louis XII of France occupies Milan and Genoa

1504 Ferdinand defeats French army at Gaeta and conquers Naples

1509 Battle of Agnadello; France and the pope defeat Venice

1512 Battle of Ravenna; French capture the city of Ravenna in northeastern Italy

1513 Battle of Novara; Swiss troops force France out of Milan

1515 Battle of Marignano; King Francis I of France defeats Swiss

1522 Battle of Bicocca; Holy Roman Emperor Charles V forces French army out of Italy

1525 Battle of Pavia; Charles decisively defeats the French army

1527 Sack of Rome; Charles's forces devastate Rome

1542 France invades northern Italy

1544 Battle of Ceresole; French forces defeat the imperial army

The wars in Italy were forums for new developments in the art of warfare. When King Charles VIII of France invaded Italy in 1494, for example, he used effective new bronze cannons to devastate medieval Italian castles. On the battlefield new formations and armaments were employed. Infantry with handguns began to replace archers, inflicting heavy casualties on an enemy armed mainly with pikes. At the same time, armies grew ever larger with increasing numbers of soldiers.

SEE ALSO

- Arms and armor
- Charles V
- Dynastic wars
- France
- Italian states
- Spain

IVAN THE TERRIBLE

The first czar of Russia, Ivan IV, known as Ivan the Terrible, has a mixed and controversial reputation. On the one hand, he helped create an efficient, centralized Russian state. On the other, he committed acts of great barbarism that were possibly signs of increasing madness.

Ivan became grand duke of Muscovy (a state centered on Moscow) on December 4, 1533, when he was only three years old, after the death of his father Grand Duke Vasily III. From that moment, until 1547 when Ivan took full power, Russia's hereditary nobles—the boyars—struggled for influence and power. Ivan's mother was poisoned by boyars in 1538, leaving him even more exposed. Ivan grew up at the center of political chaos and came to deeply distrust the boyars.

Ivan took full control of government on January 16, 1547, when he was 17 years old. He was crowned czar of all Russia, the title of czar being roughly equivalent to that of emperor. Ivan's main achievement in his early years was to create an efficient state administration (*see box p. 19*). His reforms not only made Russia function more efficiently but also weakened the inherited power of the boyars. Ivan gave land and wealth—and therefore power—to those whom he considered to have served the government well.

FOREIGN POLICY

By reforming the administration of Russia, Ivan created the model of a modern state. However, he ruled in the shadow of war. In 1552 he launched a

campaign against the Tartars, Russia's traditional enemies to the east of Muscovy, and by 1556 he had conquered a broad band of territory along the length of the Volga River.

Two years later he began a campaign to conquer Livonia and so get access to the Baltic Sea, which he regarded as vital to Russia's northern maritime trade. At first the campaign was successful. However, a coalition of neighboring countries, led by Sweden and Poland, reversed Russian gains. Crimean Tartar warriors also took advantage of Russia's troubles and

Russian forces capture the Tartar stronghold of Kazan in 1552. This was the start of a successful campaign launched by Ivan to expand Russian territory eastward.

attacked Moscow in 1571, burning almost the entire city to the ground. In 1583, after 25 years of fighting, Ivan was forced to sign a humiliating peace agreement over Livonia.

As the Livonian War turned against him, Ivan executed numerous Russian commanders and nobles as traitors and even threatened in 1564 to abdicate. However, Orthodox church officials persuaded him to stay, and the cruel years of Ivan the Terrible began.

STATE WITHIN A STATE

To deal with those whom he regarded as Russia's traitorous nobles, in 1565 Ivan created the *oprichnina*, a large area in the center and north of Russia that he ruled separately from the rest of the Russian state. He raised a personal army of around 6,000 men, known as the *oprichniki*, to do his bidding. The *oprichniki* are considered to be Russia's

first secret police. With their help Ivan established a terrifying regime. He banished wealthy nobles to remote parts of Russia. He tortured and murdered at will. Thousands of people were executed in horrific ways. Some were roasted alive on spits or fried on iron skillets. Ivan would often conduct personal drunken experiments in torture in his own private residences, sometimes in the form of horrific religious services. The slaughter occurred on a great scale. In 1570 the *oprichniki* killed about 60,000 people in the city of Novgorod alone.

THE FINAL YEARS

In 1572 the *oprichnina* was dissolved. By this time Russia had descended into political and social chaos, and Ivan's personal army had been unable to protect Moscow from destruction a year earlier. Ivan returned to ruling Russia, but his mental health seemed questionable. After an argument in 1581 he stabbed to death his oldest son, also called Ivan, leaving Russia without a strong successor to the throne (his younger son, Fyodor, was mentally simple). With Ivan's position further weakened, the Russian state became ever more chaotic.

Ivan died suddenly in 1584, leaving Russia in financial ruin.

In this painting by the 19th-century Russian artist Iliya Repin Ivan holds the body of his dead son, Ivan Ivanovich. Ivan murdered his son in a rage.

CREATING A STATE

During the early years of his reign Ivan undertook a major reorganization of the Russian state to make it function more efficiently. He formed state departments like those in modern governments—each had a specific responsibility in running the country. Local districts received their own administrators, who were elected by local nobles. In 1549 an assembly—the *zemsky sobor*—was formed to debate and provide advice on government policy.

In the military Ivan established the principle that merit rather than wealth would be the deciding factor in promotion. Finally, he also empowered the Russian Orthodox church as the dominant state religion. All these measures initially gave Russia stability and order, both qualities that Ivan would later undo through his psychopathic actions.

SEE ALSO

• Orthodox church
• Romanov family
• Russia

JAPAN

In 1500 civil war raged in Japan following a period of devastation known as the Sengoku Period, or the Age of the Country at War. The rule of the shoguns (chief military commanders) had waned, and warlords fought against one another for total control of the country.

At the beginning of the 16th century Japan's feudal system had six classes. The highest class was made up of the emperor and the royal family. Although the emperor was nominal ruler, from the 12th century power rested in the hands of successive shoguns. Below the emperor were daimyo (landowning warlords) who trained only for mounted warfare and maintained their own armies of samurai warriors. The artisans and merchants in the towns formed the third class. Remaining classes included prominent farmers with taxable fields, small holders, and peasants. People in a seventh class, the *genin*, were considered outcasts. They performed unpleasant jobs such as disposing of sewage and cleaning animal hides.

DECLINE OF FEUDALISM

The feudal system gradually broke down under continual conflict among the warlords, and the country became impoverished. Emperor Go-Nara (ruled 1536–1557) lived in a wooden hut, and his coronation, traditionally funded by the samurai, was delayed by 20 years; eventually, it was paid for by the peasants. Merchants were bankrupted as Japanese and Chinese pirates brought trade to a halt. In better times the waters surrounding Japan

This 16th-century Japanese screen painting shows armorers at work. Armor worn by the warrior class of samurai in the 16th and 17th centuries was typically a series of protective metal plates interconnected by colorful, closely woven material.

were kept free of pirates by state vessels that sank or captured ships that lacked the red seal issued to genuine traders by the ruling shogun. However, sea patrols ceased as civil wars took their toll on samurai families. People began to hoard coins as insurance against further disasters, and gradually money went out of circulation. Soon there was not enough metal to mint new supplies.

RURAL UPRISINGS

Conditions in the countryside were worse: The annual tax could be up to 70 percent of the harvest. Peasants formed themselves into defense militia led by gentleman farmers trained as samurai or by *ashigaru* ("light feet")— peasants who had left their land to serve as foot soldiers in clan armies.

Others turned for help to the local Buddhist monastery, with its army of warrior monks. The peasant rebellions defeated samurai armies, humbled shoguns, and burned the capital, Kyoto. During the Single-minded Uprising and Lotus Uprising monasteries fought against one another. From 1530 to 1536 the capital Kyoto and the surrounding area were controlled by the Nichiren Buddhists. The city was sacked and burned by the rival Tendai

monks from their fortified monastery on Mount Hiei.

Oda Nobunaga (1534–1582) had become the leading warlord by 1560. Having gained the agricultural wealth of the Owari Plain in Honshu in the center of Japan through his defeat of the great warlord Imagawa Yoshimoto in 1560, he allied with the warlord of Mikawa province, Tokugawa Ieyasu (1543–1616).

CAPTURE OF KYOTO

They first supported then destroyed the remains of the old Ashikaga shogunate. Nobunaga took control of Kyoto—an important step toward the eventual

A modern view of Osaka Castle in Japan, which was begun in 1583 by general Hideyoshi Toyotomi. He planned for the castle to become the center of a unified Japan.

THE BATTLE OF NAGASHINO

Firearms arrived in Japan with the first Portuguese trading ships in 1542 or 1543. The Japanese were probably aware of Chinese handguns before this time, but Japanese society was slow to accept foreign ideas. The Portuguese trader Mendez Pinto first excited Japanese interest when he took Totitaka, lord of Tanegashima, on a duck hunt. Totitaka took shooting lessons, and within months the Japanese were constructing their own matchlock rifles, known as Tanegashima. The weapons were largely discounted until 1560, when a bullet killed a general wearing full armor.

Oda Nobunaga first used the new weapon in conflict at the Battle of Nagashino in 1575, issuing his infantry with Tanegashimas. Four soldiers kept each marksman supplied with loaded weapons, increasing the rate of fire from a low four shots an hour. The shooters were protected from counterfire by wooden posts and earthworks. During the battle Nobunaga's 3,000 marksmen decimated the elite Takeda cavalry. Nobunaga's victory changed the course of Japanese military history and altered Japanese attitudes to European technology.

This portrait of the Japanese shogun Tokugawa Ieyasu dates from 1642. Ieyasu succeeded the powerful warlord Oda Nobunaga and continued his work of unifying Japan.

Nobunaga was the first warlord to use firearms bought from European traders. During the Battle of Nagashino in 1575 he destroyed the forces of Takeda Shingen's son Katsuyori. In a landmark battle (*see box p. 21*) Nobunaga pioneered the use of firearms, altering Japanese attitudes to European technology, and moving closer to unifying Japan.

HIDEYOSHI'S RULE

After Nobunaga was assassinated in 1582, his faithful general Toyotomi Hideyoshi continued his work. By 1590 Japan was largely unified under Hideyoshi. He was determined to keep the peasants and warriors separate to make sure that there was peace. He forbade peasants from carrying or making weapons or training as samurai, and decreed that all samurai had to live in their master's castle. Peasants and merchants were not allowed to travel without permission, and every household was kept under surveillance. In 1591 Hideyoshi forbade social mobility in his Edict on Changing Status, restoring and reinforcing the feudal system.

After Hideyoshi's death in 1598 there was a power struggle between the leading warlords for control of Japan. Tokugawa Ieyasu finally won after defeating his rivals at the Battle of Sekigahara north of Kyoto in 1600. He persuaded the emperor to name him shogun, thereby establishing the Tokugawa Shogunate. Under Ieyasu's son Hidetada and his grandson Iemitsu warlords were controlled by an edict that forced them to live in the capital.

unification of Japan. Meanwhile, faced with the coalition forces of the warlord Takeda Shingen and Honganji Kennyo, a powerful Buddhist leader, Nobunaga, destroyed the Enryaku-ji Monastery near Kyoto in 1570 and then marched on Mount Hiei, razing the Tendai fortress and slaughtering its 3,000 monks in 1571.

To suppress the Buddhist rebellion, Nobunaga then also destroyed the Nichiren monks, giving their property to the Pure Land monasteries, a school that taught a form of Buddhism popular with the peasants. Later the samurai class would be encouraged to adopt the philosophical, nonpolitical Zen form of Buddhism.

MASSACRE OF THE CHRISTIANS

While the shogunate recognized the benefits of European trade and technology, Christianity was seen as a destabilizing influence. From 1612

22

THE EDO PERIOD

Tokugawa Ieyasu's rise to power marked the beginning of the Edo Period in 1603. Named for the capital of Japan, the period centered on the cultural growth of Edo (modern Tokyo). Renga poetry, in which successive linked verses of a long poem are written by different people, gave birth to a similar form of poetry called haikai, which evolved into haiku, highly formalized short poems. Architecture flourished during the period. Splendid castles, richly decorated with paintings on sliding doors and folding screens, were built. Calligraphy and delicate ceramic ink painting were perfected, while Zen philosophy, which promoted a more simplistic lifestyle, also became popular. Nearly empty rooms were considered more pleasing than those cluttered with furniture, while the garden at Ryoanji, in Kyoto, used only white sand to represent water and rocks to depict mountains. Theater also became popular. Noh and Kabuki dance dramas were performed across Japan by actors who wore masks and elaborate costumes.

Two Japanese kabuki actors perform Renjishi ("Dance of Two Lions"), in which one plays a parent lion and the other its young cub. Kabuki is a popular form of traditional Japanese theater and is said to have begun in 1596.

steps were taken to limit foreign religions. Following a rebellion by Christians (1637–1638), the Portuguese were expelled, and 37,000 Japanese Christians executed.

Foreign merchants from China and the Netherlands were allowed to continue trading with Japan, but they were confined to the island of Dejima in Nagasaki harbor, and trade was restricted to specific items such as silk. This policy of national seclusion, or *sakoku*, continued for 200 years.

Despite political wrangling of factions in the capital, the shogunate remained in the Tokugawa family. The Tokugawa shogunate lasted until 1867 and was remembered as a period of cultural achievement (*see box above*), peace, and stability.

SEE ALSO

- Arms and armor
- Colonization
- Hideyoshi Toyotomi
- Jesuits
- Missionaries
- Trade
- Warfare

JESUITS

The Jesuits, officially called the Society of Jesus, are an order of Catholic priests that played a major part in the Counter Reformation and helped shape the history of European colonialism in Asia and Latin America for over two centuries.

The founder of the order, Ignatius Loyola (1491–1556), was originally a soldier. Born into a noble Spanish family in 1491, Loyola's military career ended when he was seriously wounded in the leg while fighting against the French in 1521. During his long convalescence he read many religious books and underwent a spiritual transformation. He wrote the first draft of his *Spiritual Exercises* and then, in 1523, went on a pilgrimage to Jerusalem during which he endured many hardships. He subsequently studied at various universities in Spain and in Paris, leading a life with no material comforts and developing a reputation for holiness.

FOUNDING THE ORDER

By the early 1530s a band of six disciples had gathered around Loyola. They worked through his *Spiritual Exercises* and in 1534 joined him in taking vows of poverty, chastity, and obedience. They expected to travel as missionaries to Jerusalem or undertake whatever work the pope might require.

Unable to reach Jerusalem, in 1538 they went as ordained priests to Rome, where they decided to create an order of the church that was to be called the

Society of Jesus. The order, which received papal recognition in 1540, was unique in that its members swore total obedience to the pope—something that was to make them unpopular with many European rulers. The highest authority within the society was the general, who lived in Rome and exercised power over lesser leaders, called provincials. Loyola reluctantly became the first general.

By 1550 Loyola and his followers had formulated rules for the society. Great value was placed on education and training, and young men were

This painting of Pope Paul III and Ignatius Loyola commemorates the pope's acceptance of the Jesuit order into the church in 1540. It had taken time to persuade Paul III to do this, despite the Jesuits' vow to obey him completely.

sometimes required to study and meditate for 15 years before entering the society. The Jesuits also vowed not to hold important church positions, such as those of bishop, cardinal, or pope. Their stated tasks were to undertake missions to foreign lands to educate children and ignorant adults, and to help the sick, prisoners, people sentenced to death, and others in need.

Although the Jesuits promised to live in poverty, they often founded schools and thus became established and wealthy property owners in towns. By the time Loyola died in 1556, more than a thousand men had already joined the society.

JESUIT MISSIONS

In founding the society, Loyola planned to fight the spread of Islam on the southern and eastern edges of Europe and to convert Muslims to Christianity. However, during his life the Reformation presented a greater threat to Catholicism. Jesuits traveled around Europe, from Ireland to Germany, calling on people to reject the new form of Christianity. They also worked to reform and strengthen the Catholic church and so played a major part in the Counter Reformation.

The Jesuits journeyed to Africa and Asia. One of the first members, Francis Xavier (1506–1552), became one of the greatest Catholic missionaries, helping establish Christianity in India, Malaysia, and Japan. The Jesuits also managed to reach China, meeting with the Ming emperor in the 1580s, but had little lasting effect. In Japan they made many converts before the government began to restrict Christianity in 1612.

The Jesuits followed the Portuguese to America, where they preached against the enslavement of the native peoples in Brazil. They also played an important role in Spanish territory, preaching and building missions in an area stretching from Paraguay to southern California. At first Jesuits were allied closely with the Catholic Spanish and Portuguese monarchs, who realized that a Jesuit presence in remote regions would reinforce the legitimacy of their claim to the territory. In French Canada Jesuits also traveled to places that no other Europeans had visited; some suffered gruesome deaths at the hands of the local native population.

ENEMIES OF THE JESUITS

The Jesuits were feared or disliked by many people. The Protestants, who recognized them as one of the strongest weapons of the Counter Reformation, particularly feared them. Catholics

This painting is in the 17th-century Jesuit church of Bom Jesus in Goa, India. The church contains the remains of the missionary Francis Xavier, who worked and preached in Goa before going to Japan in 1549. He died in 1552 while waiting for an opportunity to enter China.

also disliked them for a variety of reasons. The Jesuits were powerful and answered to no secular leaders. They were also often very successful in their ventures. In Brazil, for example, they owned the most prosperous sugar plantation.

SUCCESS IN PARAGUAY

A source of great pride to the Jesuits in the Americas was their success in the area now called Paraguay, where they virtually ruled over their own country, populated by thousands of native converts. The Jesuits educated their converts and built beautiful churches. However, in the 18th century the monarchs of both Portugal and Spain came to see the Jesuits as a threat to their own power in the Americas.

Eventually the Portuguese decided to expel the Jesuits from their empire. In 1758 Portuguese colonial officials used brutal force to drive the Jesuits out of Brazil. The Spanish soon followed suit, and in 1773 the pope made the entire Society of Jesus illegal. Although some Jesuits practiced in Russia after the ban, most of them became ordinary priests. However, in 1814 the society was restored by a later pope; the Jesuits continue with missionary and educational work to the present day.

Three Jesuit priests are killed by native inhabitants of Chile in 1612. In remote areas in South America many Jesuits became the victims of the people they sought to convert.

JESUITS AND AFRICAN SLAVES

From Mexico to Brazil the Jesuits owned slaves to work their prosperous plantations. However, in Cartagena, an important port city on the Caribbean coast of South America, Jesuits in the 17th century made it their mission to convert and baptize thousands of people destined to be sold as slaves as they arrived after the long journey across the Atlantic Ocean from Africa. The Jesuits greeted the sick, depressed, and angry new arrivals in the holds of slave ships by giving them water, fruit, candy, and other gifts to win their trust and confidence. They then preached Christian beliefs to the Africans in the hope that they would willingly choose to be baptized or that they would become Catholics before being sold as slaves.

One of these missionaries to the African slaves, Peter Claver (1581–1654), was made a saint in the Catholic church. Centuries later Jesuits in the United States used the story of this saint when preaching to African American freedmen.

SEE ALSO

- Baroque
- Colonization
- Counter Reformation
- Latin America
- Missionaries
- Religious orders
- Schools and schooling

JEWS AND JUDAISM

At the beginning of the 16th century there were Jewish communities throughout Europe, West Asia and North Africa, and in many parts of Asia, including India and China. By the end of the 17th century Jews had also begun to settle in North and South America.

The situation of Jews varied greatly over the course of the 16th and 17th centuries and from region to region. The period began catastrophically for the Jews of Spain. In 1492 all Jews except those who converted to Christianity were expelled from the country. Perhaps 20,000 Jewish families went into exile.

The few Jews who remained outwardly accepted Catholicism while often secretly practicing Judaism. Known as Marranos, they ran the risk of being denounced to the Catholic court known as the Inquisition. If they were found guilty, they could be burned alive. In 1496 the Jews were also driven out of Portugal.

NEW COMMUNITIES
Jews exiled from Spain and Portugal and their descendants became known as Sephardim for the Hebrew word for Spain. Some went to Italy, England, and the Netherlands, but most found refuge in North Africa and the eastern Mediterranean, especially in the Ottoman Empire, which from 1516 included present-day Israel. The centers of Jewish population there were Jerusalem and Safed in Galilee, where there was a great flowering of the kabbalah, a Jewish mystical tradition.

Some Jews in Ottoman Turkey rose to positions of power and influence. For example, Don Joseph Nasi, a wealthy merchant form Portugal, was created a duke by Ottoman Sultan Selim II (ruled 1566–1574). Nasi planned to establish an independent Jewish

Moses Haman (1490–1554), who is portrayed in this engraving, was personal physician, adviser, and friend to the Ottoman Sultan Suleyman the Magnificent (ruled 1520–1566). The Ottomans welcomed Jews and sent ships from Istanbul in the 1490s to collect those expelled from Spain and Portugal.

community in Tiberias, but he fell from favor before they could be carried out. Many Sephardic exiles settled in Thessaloniki, Greece, then also part of the Ottoman Empire. The city became one of the world's largest Jewish communities in the 16th century.

As in the Middle Ages, Jews were subjected to persecution throughout Europe in the Reformation period. Anti-Semitism, or prejudice against Jews, had led to periodic persecution on the pretext that they were collectively responsible for the death of Christ. They were also accused of usury—the sin of making a dishonest profit—since many moneylenders were Jews.

In Germany Jews were expelled from several towns. German reformer Martin Luther demanded that they either be used as forced labor or expelled. From the 1650s, however, conditions improved. Many German states, having suffered heavy losses in the Thirty Years' War (1618–1648), employed Jews to fill a wide range of vacant jobs. The Jews took this opportunity to reestablish some of the communities that had been destroyed during the Reformation.

EASTERN EUROPE

German Jews were educated by devout scholars, rabbis, and teachers who came mainly from Poland–Lithuania. Jewish scholarship flourished there in the 16th century as the Jews were given official privileges. Polish Jews created local and regional self-governing political bodies. The most important of these was the Jewish Council of Four Lands—Great Poland, Little Poland, Polish Russia (Podolia-Galicia), and Volhynia. The Czech city of Prague was also a center of Jewish culture and learning.

From the mid-16th century Jews spread out from Poland to parts of Russia and Ukraine. Here they were routinely persecuted and often forced to convert to Orthodox Christianity. In 1648 around 100,000 Jews who had settled in Ukraine were massacred by Cossacks. Some years later Muscovite armies captured various cities in present-day Belarus and Lithuania, and killed all Jews that they found there.

THE ITALIAN STATES

The Jews who had left Spain for Italy were joined there in the late 16th century by North African Jews from Turkey and Palestine. From 1516 the Jews in Venice were forced to live in a segregated area called the ghetto. This practice spread to other Italian states.

This illuminated manuscript dating from 1604 was a product of the kabbalah. An ancient Jewish mystical tradition, the kabbalah is based on an obscure interpretation of the Old Testament.

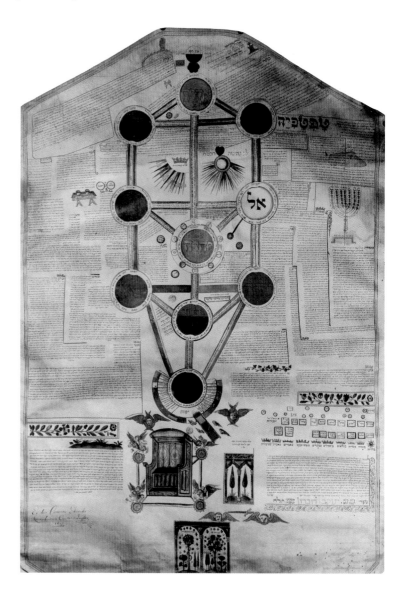

Under Pope Pius V (pope 1566–1572) Jews were expelled from most Papal States. Those who remained were taxed heavily and barred from many jobs. As a result, in 1698 the Roman Jewish community was forced into bankruptcy.

However, Jews were able to take part more fully in the life of Italy than in that of almost any other country. Jewish scholars wrote in both Hebrew and Italian, producing a wide range of literary works as well as books on astronomy, philosophy, and history. They were bankers, doctors, musicians, gold- and silversmiths, and merchants. Italian rabbis made major contributions to the *Halakhah* (the laws of Judaism based on oral traditions).

JEWS IN NORTHERN EUROPE

The Jewish community in England had been expelled in 1290, but they began to return after the start of the Spanish Inquisition. In 1656 Oliver Cromwell, lord protector of England, formally welcomed back the Jews. He correctly thought that the presence of the Jews would stimulate international trade.

Much of the ensuing commerce came to England from the Netherlands, where many Spanish and Portuguese Jews had settled. In the 17th century the increasing freedoms that Jews had been granted, especially in Antwerp and Amsterdam, attracted further Jewish immigration, this time from eastern Europe. A business community emerged that took an active part in the exploration and settlement of Dutch colonies in the Americas, and the East Indies. Dutch Jews excelled as artists, physicians, and writers in both Spanish and Portuguese. A well-known Dutch Jew of the time was the philosopher Baruch Spinoza (1632–1677), the son of Portuguese immigrants.

In France the Jews of Provence were expelled in 1501 on the orders of King Louis XII (ruled 1498–1515). Those who converted to Christianity were allowed to remain, but from 1512 they were subjected to punitive taxation. However, the anti-Semitism of the French, like that of the Germans, was moderated by the Thirty Years' War. When France took control of the province of Alsace under the terms of the 1648 Treaty of Westphalia, resident Jews were encouraged to stay and fill vacant jobs. France even began to encourage Jewish immigration, which attracted survivors from Ukraine.

THE "PROMISED LAND"

Widely dispersed, Jewish communities cherished hopes of a great leader or messiah who would unite them and take them back to the Promised Land in Palestine. Several people claimed to be the messiah during this period.

The most influential false messiah was a Turkish-born Jew called Sabbatai Zebi. In 1665 he declared himself to be the messiah. His claims caused great excitement, and he gained many followers. Faith in Zebi was dashed when, on pain of death, he converted to Islam in 1666. However, he inspired a sect that continued after his death.

A Jewish school is depicted in this 17th-century Dutch painting. Many Spanish and Portuguese Jews settled in Holland and became important figures in the business and literary worlds.

SEE ALSO
- Ottoman Empire
- Religious dissent
- Spain
- Spinoza, Baruch

K'ANG-HSI

K'ang-hsi (1654–1722) was the second emperor of the Manchu Ch'ing Dynasty, the last imperial dynasty in China. One of the greatest rulers in China's history, he ruled from 1661, extending the area under Manchu control and promoting the arts and sciences.

The Ch'ing ("Pure") Dynasty was established in the early 17th century by the Manchu, tribal peoples from Manchuria (in what is now northeastern China) who had united in the second half of the 16th century under the leadership of Nurhachi (1559–1626), K'ang-hsi's great grandfather. The foreign Ch'ing Dynasty succeeded largely because the Manchus, who made up only a tiny fraction of the population, adopted many aspects of Chinese culture and employed Chinese officials in both central and local government.

THE EARLY YEARS

K'ang-hsi inherited the throne when he was only six years old. Consequently four regents ran the government on his behalf until 1667, when, at the age of 13, K'ang-hsi assumed leadership and expelled the regents. He also began to father children, eventually producing a reported 56 children by 30 consorts.

K'ang-hsi believed that his power rested on the welfare and good will of his subjects, and he made a great effort to ensure honesty in his government and to foster good relations between the Chinese and the Manchu. He made six tours of inspection around the

country to see for himself what conditions were like and watched carefully over the economy, sponsoring water-conservation projects that helped agriculture flourish and reducing taxes

Emperor K'ang-hsi, whose name means Peaceful Harmony, ruled China for 61 years.

when necessary. He recruited Chinese administrators and officials through competitive examinations.

A SPONSOR OF LEARNING

K'ang-hsi was a scholar who was familiar with the Chinese classics and wrote good-quality literary prose and poetry. He believed that learning was the foundation of good government and was one of the greatest sponsors of learning in Chinese imperial history.

One measure he took was to employ Jesuit missionaries to map the Chinese Empire and to teach mathematics and astronomy. K'ang-hsi learned Latin from the missionaries so that he could correspond with European rulers and popes. He encouraged literature, art, printing, and porcelain production. Among the works he patronized were a history of the Ming Dynasty and a massive 5,000-volume encyclopedia on China's cultural heritage. He was fascinated by clocks and built a large collection of them.

K'ang-hsi was a determined military leader. Early in his reign he suppressed the Rebellion of the Three Feudatories

(1673–1681). These were largely independent territories in southern China that had been granted to three Chinese warlords who had helped the Manchu come to power. K'ang-hsi used diplomatic as well as military means to eliminate the warlords.

Later in his reign he conquered Taiwan (1683), established diplomatic relations with Russia (1689), and defeated the Mongols in 1696 and 1697, incorporating Outer Mongolia into the Chinese Empire.

K'ang-hsi encouraged the production of fine porcelain, such as this shaving bowl, which was made to be sold in Europe. The emperor was a great supporter of trade between China and Europe.

THE SACRED EDICTS

In 1670, when Emperor K'ang-hsi was 16, he issued a list of Sacred Edicts to be read twice a month in every village and town of the empire to guide his subjects on how to behave to ensure their goodness, happiness, and prosperity. These are some of the edicts:

• *Maintain good relations in the neighborhood to prevent quarrels and lawsuits.*
• *Be moderate and economical in order to avoid wasting away your livelihood.*
• *Make the most of schools and academies in order to honor the ways of scholars.*

• *Show propriety and courtesy to improve customs and manners.*
• *Work hard in your professions in order to quiet your ambitions.*
• *Instruct sons and younger brothers in order to prevent their committing any wrong.*
• *Put a stop to false accusations in order to protect the good and honest.*
• *Promptly and fully pay your taxes in order to avoid forced requisition.*
• *Free yourself from resentment and anger in order to show respect for your body and your life.*

SEE ALSO

• Central Asia
• China
• Jesuits
• Porcelain

KIEV

The fortress city of Kiev was founded in about 860 A.D. on the eastern bank of the Dnieper River, in what is now Ukraine. In the 16th century it was a possession of Poland–Lithuania, while in the 17th century it came under the rule of Muscovy.

Most of the city of Kiev was destroyed by a Mongol army in 1240. What was left was captured by the Grand Duchy of Lithuania in 1362. Although it was the seat of a metropolitan (Orthodox bishop), Kiev had little significance other than as a small market town on the frontier between Lithuania and the Tartars in the Crimea.

Kiev suffered repeated attacks by the Crimean Tartars, who captured and sacked the city in 1482. In 1516, in an attempt to stimulate Kiev's trade and so help it recover, Grand Duke Sigismund I granted it a charter of autonomy.

A POLISH POSSESSION

Since the 14th century the states of Lithuania and Poland had been closely linked. In Poland the Jesuits had been very effective in spreading Catholicism. As Polish influence reached Kiev, the city became a center of Orthodox opposition to Roman Catholicism.

An Orthodox brotherhood was established to oppose the Jesuits and encourage Ukrainian nationalism. Peter Mogila, the metropolitan of Kiev from 1633 to 1646, founded the Collegium, which became the rallying point of anti-Catholicism.

In the 17th century Kiev was drawn into the battle between the Polish king and the Zaporozhian Cossacks, who lived on the banks of the Dnieper River. In 1648 the Cossack leader Bohdan Khmelnytsky led the Cossacks and Tartars in an uprising.

Khmelnytsky captured Kiev, which welcomed him as a defender of the Orthodox faith. The Poles besieged the city, and in 1654 Khmelnytsky had to sign the Pereyaslav Agreement with the Russians. This effectively granted Kiev and Ukraine to Muscovy, the leading state in Russia.

The citizens resisted this settlement, and conflict dragged on until 1667, when a treaty was signed. Kiev and lands to the east of the Dnieper became an independent Cossack state, while remaining under Muscovy's protection. There followed a period of struggle against the Turks, during which the Cossacks frequently changed sides and fought among themselves. In 1686 Kiev finally came fully under Muscovy's rule.

Kiev is sometimes known as the "gold-domed city" because of its many Orthodox churches. It was a very important center of Orthodox opposition to Catholicism in the 16th and 17th centuries.

SEE ALSO

• Orthodox church
• Poland–Lithuania
• Russia

LANGUAGE

The enormous changes in Europe between 1500 and 1700, especially the advent of printing, had a great effect on language development. Influenced by the languages of the new lands encountered on voyages of exploration Europeans themselves changed.

The development of printing in the mid-15th century led to the production of multiple copies of books in different languages. The first printed books in most languages were religious texts, often Bible translations.

The availability of printed books helped standardize languages and also ironed out regional variations. The process often resulted in one language or dialect prevailing over others. In Germany, for example, Martin Luther intended his translation of the Bible to be in a form most German-speaking people could understand. Luther based his translation on the German of the court of Saxony, which thus laid the foundation for standard German. In England the Authorized Version of the Bible, published in 1611, and the fact that most printers were London-based meant that the southern dialect became standard English.

In France the dialect of Paris and its surrounding region gradually became the standard. King Francis I decreed in 1539 that it should be the official language throughout the kingdom. The royal proclamation marginalized not only other dialects of French but also other languages spoken in France: Basque, Breton, Flemish, and Occitan.

Y BEIBL CYS-
SEGR-LAN. SEF
YR HEN DESTA-
MENT, A'R NEWYDD.

2. *Timoth.* 3. 14, 15.

Eithr aros di yn y pethau a ddyfcaift, ac a ymddyried-
wyd i ti, gan wybod gan bwy y dyfcaift.
Ac i ti er yn fachgen wybod yr fcrythur lân, yr hon
fydd abl i'th wneuthur yn ddoeth i iechydwria-
eth, trwy'r ffydd yr hon fydd yng-Hrift Iefu.

Imprinted at London by the Deputies of
CHRISTOPHER BARKER,
Printer to the Queenes moft excel-
lent Maieftie.

1588.

DECLINE OF LATIN

Latin had been the Europe-wide language of science and philosophy in the Middle Ages. In the 14th century, however, Renaissance humanists began to focus on the development of local languages and their literature. In 1441 a poetry competition was set up in Italy

The title page of the first Welsh translation of the Bible, published in 1588. The first printed book in many languages was the Bible.

to improve the standard of the Italian language and to show that it was not inferior to Latin. In 1553 a group of French poets set up a movement to encourage writing in French, rather than Latin, and to establish a modern French literature. Their work was continued by chief minister Cardinal Richelieu, who founded the French Literary Academy in 1635 to maintain the purity of the French language.

At the same time, Latin was being increasingly sidelined as the language of scientific communication. Leading scientists such as Galileo Galilei and Isaac Newton began to publish their discoveries in their own language so that their ideas would be read by the general public beyond the scientific community. In addition, the split caused by the Reformation resulted in church services in Protestant countries being held in local languages rather than Latin. However, Catholics continued to use Latin extensively.

BIRTH OF MODERN ENGLISH

Modern English dates from around 1500. It differs in several ways from the previous form, known as Middle English. One major difference is in pronunciation. Nobody knows why, but between 1400 and 1800 there was a gradual change in English pronunciation called the Great Vowel Shift. The change was particularly rapid in the 15th and 16th centuries. Words such as "five" and "life" were pronounced as "feef" and "leef" in Middle English. "Sheep" was pronounced "shape." In the 16th century it became clear that spelling needed to change, since the way words were written no longer corresponded to the way they were pronounced. The first attempts to reform English spelling began at this time. The movement continues today.

Another feature of modern English was the adoption of many words from Latin and Greek by scholars as a result of the revival of interest in classical languages. The spread of printing also had an enormous effect on standardizing English.

The growth of trade brought increased contact between the nations within Europe, while worldwide European exploration led to contact with many new peoples and cultures.

Trading was one reason for Europeans to communicate with local peoples.

These developments heralded a period of vigorous cross-fertilization among different languages.

As Europeans came across animals, plants, and geographical features they had never seen before, they often adopted local words for them. So, for example, "chocolate" comes from the Aztec word *xocolatl*, and "puma" is a loan word from a language spoken in what is now Paraguay.

As Europeans sailed west across the Atlantic, meanwhile, the Americas were colonized by European languages. English first reached North America with John Cabot in 1497; a year later Christopher Columbus introduced Spanish to mainland South America.

The English-speaking colonists in North America created their own distinct dialect. Some words that fell out of use in England itself were preserved in this dialect, such as "fall" for "autumn" and "trash" for "rubbish." American English also adopted words from Native American languages, such as raccoon, hickory, and canoe.

Although English became the principal language of North America, in the meantime it faced competition from the languages of other settlers: Basque, Dutch, French, German, and Spanish. The growth in the slave trade brought the languages of Akan, Wolof, and Yoruba from West Africa.

PIDGINS AND CREOLES

Pidgin languages developed to allow people who had no common language to communicate with each other. A pidgin combines elements of two or more languages for simple communication. In 1542 the French explorer Jacques Cartier found that the Native Americans of the St. Lawrence Basin already spoke a form of Basque; in 17th-century Quebec traders used a mix of French and Algonquian.

The first English traders in India discovered they needed Portuguese or an Indian-Portuguese pidgin to talk to the local population.

Pidgins are strictly practical; if they develop a more complex form and a richer vocabulary used for conversation and the expression of abstract ideas, they are known as creoles. The most famous creole in North America is Louisiana Creole, which derives from a mix of French and African languages.

Pidgins and creoles often developed on tropical islands, such as in the Caribbean. In this region and many other colonial outposts native peoples were soon learning three languages: their own mother tongue, the settlers' language, and the creole that had started as a pidgin bridge between the other two.

LOAN WORDS

The Reformation period was also rich in loan words, borrowings by one language from another when they came into contact. The Italian Wars in the 16th century led to about 800 Italian words passing into French, mainly of two types: one derived from the arts, such as *fugue* and *opéra*, and the other from military terms, such as *colonel* and *soldat*. French wars with Spain in the 17th century also increased French vocabulary by about 200 words.

The French king Louis XIV (ruled 1643–1715) gives an audience to the pope's nephew, specially sent to apologize for an insult to the French ambassador in Rome. French diplomatic skill in the 17th-century led to French being adopted as the language of international diplomacy.

SEE ALSO

- Bibles and bible studies
- Colonization
- Education
- Humanism
- Literacy
- Printing

LATIN AMERICA

Latin America is a term now used to refer to regions that became colonies of Spain and Portugal following the discovery of the West Indies by Columbus in 1492. It includes some islands in the Caribbean Sea, Mexico, and the countries of Central America and South America.

The term "Latin America" did not exist until the 19th century, when it was coined by France in an attempt to strengthen connections between the French colonies and the Spanish- and Portuguese-speaking countries of the Americas. The Spanish and Portuguese were the first Europeans to settle in the Americas. They did so in the 16th century,

regarding themselves as pioneers in distant kingdoms under the dominion of the monarchs of Spain and Portugal.

England, the Netherlands, and France established colonies in the 17th century, by which time there had been a drastic reduction in the numbers of native people. It is estimated that between 1520 and 1650 the native population in Spanish and Portuguese

Mexico City, shown in this plan dating from 1628, was built on the site of the Aztec capital city, Tenochtitlán. It was the capital of Spanish America for 300 years.

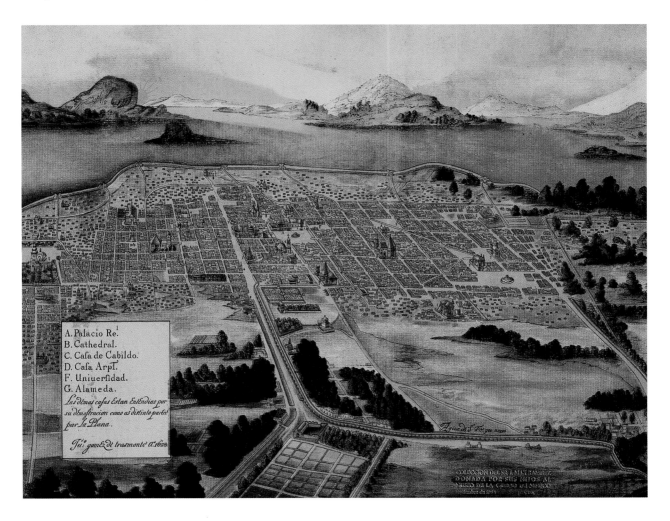

A. Palacio Re.¹
B. Cathedral.
C. Cafa de Cabildo.
D. Cafa Arpt.
F. Uniuerfidad.
G. Alameda.
Las dℓmas cafas Eftan Enℓndias por
su dℓmostracion como as distinto partes
por la Plana.

Jℓi: gomℓ ∂ℓ trasmonte a.1628.

America was reduced by 90 percent, mainly because of a lack of resistance to diseases brought over the Atlantic. These included diseases from Africa, since from the beginning of the 16th century Africans were brought to Latin America to work on the plantations and in the mines as slaves. About 500,000 slaves were imported by the Spanish and Portuguese colonies between 1500 and 1650.

THE SPANISH COLONIES

Christopher Columbus's 1492 discovery of the West Indies on behalf of Spain was quickly followed by further exploration and the setting up of colonies. Spanish adventurers came to the Americas seeking great fortunes. However, the Spanish crown would not allow these adventurers to become rulers of the lands they had conquered. Instead, in a relatively short time colonial governments put power into the hands of government officials.

The most important government official in Spanish America was the viceroy (meaning "vice king"), who ruled over large territories in the name of the monarch. For around 200 years only two viceroyalties existed in Spanish America: the Viceroyalty of New Spain and the Viceroyalty of Peru. The Viceroyalty of New Spain extended from what is now California south to Central America, with its capital at Mexico City. The Viceroyalty of Peru included almost all of South America apart from Brazil, which was Portuguese. The viceroy ruled from Lima, a city founded by the Spanish on the coast of Peru.

In addition to the viceroys there were many Spanish officials at a more local level controlling the regions and towns. They enforced laws through several kinds of courts, including courts for trying criminals, courts for civil

A richly dressed Spanish overseer at the Potosí silver mine poses on horseback in this 17th-century painting. Potosí, in present-day Bolivia, was the largest silver mine in the Spanish Empire and a major source of the bullion that poured into Spain from the second half of the 16th century.

cases, courts connected to the church that dealt with issues such as divorce, and the courts of the Inquisition, which dealt with heresy and other crimes against the Catholic church.

Although the Spanish claimed a vast area of the Americas, they really only controlled and settled isolated regions. The native people of southern Chile, for example, continued to resist Spanish military attacks until the 1800s. Even today some people in Latin America speak local languages, not Spanish and Portuguese.

THE ROLE OF THE CHURCH

In many areas of Latin America the only Spanish speakers whom the native peoples met were priests and missionaries of the Catholic church. They played a major role in bringing Spanish culture to the Americas, thus making sure that the majority of the population adopted Catholicism.

It was often the case that the only people who were willing, inspired, and motivated to go to small villages and remote regions in the Spanish Empire were the members of missionary religious orders, such as Franciscan and Dominican friars or the Fathers of the Society of Jesus (Jesuits). Soon after Hernán Cortés conquered the Aztec Empire in 1521, a dozen Franciscan friars arrived in Mexico, thinking of themselves as 12 apostles. They and the religious orders that followed them divided up the territory of Spanish America among themselves and preached Christianity wherever they could find possible converts. From the mid-16th century missionaries—in particular the Jesuits—were also active in the Portuguese colony of Brazil.

PORTUGUESE INFLUENCE

Portugal acquired Brazil as a result of the pope's declaration in 1493 that all lands to the west of an arbitrary line drawn down the middle of the Atlantic Ocean were Spanish, while those to the east were Portuguese. In the late 15th century the Portuguese kings were most interested in establishing trading posts and acquiring territory east of the line, in Africa, India, and China—regions that promised great wealth. Brazil also lay east of the line, but the Portuguese kings took little interest in this area.

For more than a century the Portuguese government divided Brazil into parcels of land that it awarded to military captains and nobles in search of riches. Ships from several European nations landed on Brazil's coast, collecting valuable brazil wood and other exotic products of the jungle, which were delivered to the coast by native traders.

The situation changed toward the end of the 1500s, when the Portuguese realized that sugar plantations offered the best profits from Brazil's tropical climate and soil. At first native people

This map of Brazil was produced in the 1660s, a time when the majority of Portuguese settlers lived on sugar plantations, such as the one illustrated here.

worked on the plantations. However, coming from cultures with little experience of settled agriculture, their productivity was low; many also died because of their lack of resistance to European diseases. The Portuguese began to take advantage of their outposts on the west coast of Africa to send slaves from the Congo and what is now Angola to Brazil to cut sugarcane and process it into sugar and rum.

The northeastern region produced much of the colony's wealth in sugar until the end of the 17th century, and most Portuguese colonists settled in this area. From around 1700, however, Portuguese settlements appeared in the south following the discovery there of gold, diamonds, and emeralds. The Portuguese did not settle much beyond the Atlantic coast of Brazil for the entire time they ruled the territory.

SPANISH TREASURE

Unlike the Portuguese, the Spanish had been intent on mining the gold and silver in their American territories from the moment they were discovered. The conquest of the Aztec and Inca empires in Mexico and Peru produced a great deal of gold, already mined and made into jewelry and decorations. The Spanish even dreamed of finding El Dorado, a lake full of gold, because of rumors they had heard of a local ritual in which every year large quantities of gold were thrown into a lake.

Although the Spanish never discovered El Dorado, they did find several mountains full of silver. The most famous of these was the Rich Mountain of San Luis Potosí, a mine located in the highlands of what is now Bolivia. Potosí was one of the most populous cities in the world in the late 1500s and early 1600s, but only a small number of Spaniards op lived there because it was at an altitude of

CARTAGENA

Cartagena, on the Caribbean coast of Colombia, was once a center for international trade between Spain and its colonies in South America. It was founded in 1534, and residents survived for the first few decades by using African slaves to pillage nearby burial sites of the indigenous people, which were full of gold objects. As a rich trading town, and one of only two official port cities in Spanish South America, Cartagena was frequently attacked by pirates, including the British seaman Francis Drake, whom Cartagena residents called "the Dragon." An immense wall was soon built around the city, as well as a fort, to provide protection against attacks. About once a year Spanish fleets entered the port, trading European goods for gold and silver mined in South America. Cartagena had a large slave market: A few thousand African slaves arrived in the city each year after several months at sea. It also became famous for its Inquisition court—where residents were put on trial for witchcraft, heresy, and blasphemy—and its contraband trade, which probably provided the region with more goods from England and France than did the legal trade with Spain.

The port of Cartagena is illustrated in this engraving of 1700.

14,000 feet (4,270m). Local and African slaves mined and processed the silver, which was then loaded onto ships bound for Spain. The riches in America kept the colonial economy moving, financing many wars between Spain and its enemies in Europe.

SEE ALSO

- Aztec Empire
- Conquistadors
- Inca Empire
- Spanish Empire

LAWS AND THE JUDICIAL SYSTEM

Laws and the judiciary, the system of courts that administer justice, are of fundamental importance to government and the maintenance of law and order. As European nations became increasingly centralized in the 1500s and 1600s, their legal systems developed accordingly.

By the 1500s the monarchs of most European countries governed their subjects and maintained peace and order within their realms through a system of what is known as civil law. This system was based on a number of sources, the most important of which was Roman law, the comprehensive legal framework that the ancient Romans had developed to govern their empire. This law was modified by later legal traditions and practices, including those of Germanic peoples, the Catholic church, the feudal system, and the laws used to regulate commerce. Roman law remained

A magistrate reads a contract to two peasants in this painting by the 17th-century Flemish artist Paul de Vos.

particularly influential in Italy, which had been at the center of the empire, and in Germany, where the Holy Roman emperors regarded themselves as inheritors of Roman traditions. Scholarly interest in Roman law had been revived at Bologna University in the 11th century, and the teaching of Roman law spread to other universities in Europe to satisfy the demand for trained judges and administrators created by the growing governments of many countries.

COMMON LAW

A different system, common law, developed in England. It later became the basis of the legal system adopted in the English colonies in North America in the 17th century. Common law had its origins in Anglo-Saxon times (fifth–11th centuries); and although it was influenced by Roman law, it developed in a different way. Much common law was customary law, which means that it was built up from the results of earlier legal cases rather than by statutes (laws) issued by the government—although statutes were increasingly used in the 15th and 16th centuries. The emphasis on customary law was fostered by the Inns of Court in London, organizations that dominated the training of legal professionals and the practice of law. Unlike the theoretical education delivered at universities, the Inns of Court gave a practical, on-the-job training in law and emphasized study of past cases.

THE ENGLISH JUSTICE SYSTEM

There were two principal systems for dispensing justice in England: the common-law courts and the courts of equity. The exercise of common law throughout the realm depended mainly on justices of the peace (JPs), also called magistrates. They were usually

STANDING TRIAL

In England people suspected of crimes were brought before a justice of the peace (JP), who decided whether there was enough evidence to take the matter further. If the offense was a minor one, such as petty theft, the JP dealt with it in a court called the Petty Session. People found guilty were sentenced to punishments such as public whipping, which were intended to cause them shame and pain. If the crime was more serious, the JP ordered the suspect to appear at the next Quarter Session, a court that met four times a year. There a prosecutor presented the charges against the accused person to a grand jury composed of people who were the social equal of the accused. The jury heard witnesses' statements and then voted on whether there was enough evidence to send the case to trial. If they voted yes, the accused person was indicted (charged) and had to plead either guilty or not guilty. If the crime was serious, the accused person was sent for trial at an assize court (a court held periodically in certain towns and presided over by a judge) or to one of three common-law courts in London. The trial was held before a grand jury, and witnesses for the prosecution and the defense gave testimony in turn, presenting evidence that could include hearsay. The jury then conferred and delivered its verdict; the presiding judge could overturn the jury's decision. If the accused person was found guilty, he or she was sentenced to punishment. Many crimes were punishable by death, often by tortuous means such as being hanged, drawn, and quartered.

A defendant is called to the bar of a courtroom to enter a plea of guilty or not guilty in this late 17th-century illustration.

important landowners who were not paid for their duties and had no legal training. When in court, they received advice from legally qualified clerks. JPs administered justice on a local level and referred more serious cases to courts of assize or one of the common-law courts in London (*see box p. 41*). In the English justice system people were considered innocent until proven guilty.

The courts of equity initially developed to deal with cases that could not be resolved in common-law courts, or which people felt had been handled unfairly in those courts. They consisted of the Court of Chancery, Court of Star Chamber, Court of Requests, Court of the Admiralty, and Court of High Commission. They took their authority directly from the monarch and therefore had almost unlimited jurisdiction and powers. All operated without using juries.

By the early 17th century the Court of Chancery and the Court of Star Chamber were attracting growing opposition. Some people saw them as a challenge to the common-law courts and as the instruments of unjust royal power. The Court of Star Chamber, which had grown out of the medieval king's council, became a symbol of oppression when King Charles I (ruled 1625–1649) used it to enforce unpopular political and ecclesiastical policies. It was abolished in 1641.

ARMS OF THE LAW
In most European countries there were no paid police officers to enforce the law in the 1500s and 1600s. It was the duty of every citizen to maintain the peace of the realm and to assist in the capture of suspected criminals. In English towns and villages voluntary parish constables were appointed who had special duties to maintain law and order. Only in France did a centralized

system of paid police officers begin to develop under King Louis XIV (ruled 1643–1715). Louis oversaw the creation of a number of different officers and organizations to carry out policing duties in Paris.

INTERNATIONAL LAW
The laws and judicial systems of European countries developed as these nations became more centralized. At the same time, several legal thinkers began to focus on questions relating to international law—the codes of behavior that should govern all people regardless of nationality. They were spurred on by the exploration and colonization of new lands, the increase in maritime trade, and the devastating potential of warfare.

Thinkers such as the Dutch jurist Hugo Grotius (1583–1645) began to move away from the earlier emphasis on the law of war to focus instead on how states should conduct relations with each other during times of peace.

Two officers patrol the streets of Paris in this 19th-century print. They are members of two early police forces: that of the Lieutenant of the Short Robe, which dealt with violent crime in Paris, and that of the Provost of the Ile de France, which patrolled the city's suburbs.

SEE ALSO
- Crime and punishment
- Daily life
- Diplomacy
- Heresy and heretics
- Inquisition
- Pirates and brigands
- Religious dissent

LEIBNIZ, GOTTFRIED

The German philosopher, scientist, educator, mathematician, and lawyer Gottfried Wilhelm Leibniz (1646–1716) was one of the outstanding intellects of his age. He was a wide-ranging thinker who made contributions in many different areas of knowledge.

Leibniz was the only great philosopher of his age who was obliged to earn his living. He worked variously as a lawyer and counselor to nobility, a geological engineer, a librarian, and a historian.

Leibniz entered the university in Leipzig at age 15 and became a doctor of law at age 20. He then began an eventful life that took him from the courts of Germany and Russia to the mines of the Harz Mountains, where he helped found the science of geology and designed practical machines such as wind-powered water pumps.

IDEAS AND ACHIEVEMENTS

Leibniz thought that the universe was composed of spiritual entities called monads, which gave the appearance of a physical world—an idea similar to modern physicists' view that the universe can be reduced to atoms that are themselves just bundles of energy. With René Descartes (1596–1650) and Baruch Spinoza (1632–1677) Leibniz belonged to the rationalist tradition of thinkers who believed that knowledge about the world comes not just from our senses but also from the power of deductive reasoning.

Leibniz was a great mathematician as well as a philosopher. In 1673 he constructed a calculating machine. By 1675 his studies had led him to lay the foundations of integral and differential calculus independently of Isaac Newton (1642–1727). He also contributed to the branch of mathematics known as topology, an extension of geometry.

Leibniz tried to reconcile the science of his day with the ideas of the ancient Greek philosopher Aristotle. He also aimed to unite the Protestant and Catholic churches. However, both of these projects were doomed to failure. Leibniz died in Germany in 1716.

Leibniz looks confidently out from this portrait. He was recognized as a great thinker in his own day and was remarkable for the breadth of his studies and ideas.

SEE ALSO

- Descartes, René
- Mathematics
- Newton, Isaac
- Philosophy
- Spinoza, Baruch

LEPANTO, BATTLE OF

The Battle of Lepanto on October 7, 1571, was the first major defeat the Ottoman Turks had experienced in 200 years. Outgunned and outmaneuvered by superior European ships, the Ottoman fleet was devastated in the Mediterranean off the coast of Greece.

From 1500 the Ottoman rulers sought to extend their control in the eastern Mediterranean. After capturing Rhodes in 1522, the island of Cyprus, then controlled by Venice, became its next target. In 1570 a large Ottoman invasion force headed for the island. By August Cyprus was in Ottoman hands despite the Venetian forces putting up a brave fight. The defeat shocked Europe, and Venice quickly formed an alliance with Pope Pius V and King Philip II of Spain to respond to the invasion.

ALLIED RESPONSE

The pope and the king assembled a naval force known as the Holy League, made up of ships from Venice, Spain, Malta, and Hapsburg countries. Philip's half-brother Don John of Austria, an illegitimate son of Holy Roman Emperor Charles V, was commander of the fleet. The fleet set sail in 1571, numbering 208 vessels. The Ottoman navy had a larger force of 270 ships, but they relied mainly on ramming to sink the enemy, whereas the league's vessels used cannons. In total they had 1,815 cannons to the Turks' 750.

The two fleets met off Lepanto (Navpaktos) in western Greece, where the massive firepower of the league's vessels soon overwhelmed the Turks. The league also had powerful three-masted ships known as galleasses that carried more guns. These caused havoc among the Turkish vessels, destroying them with crushing broadsides (when a ship turns sideways to the enemy to fire all its cannons at the same time).

When the battle was over, up to 200 of the Ottoman vessels were either sunk or captured. The league lost only 15 ships. The battle was seen as a great victory throughout Europe, although the Ottomans soon rebuilt their navy and held onto Cyprus. However, their influence in the Mediterranean had been reduced.

This contemporary painting shows a scene from the Battle of Lepanto in 1571. During the conflict an allied Christian naval force devastated a larger Ottoman fleet.

SEE ALSO

- Italian states
- Naval power
- Ottoman Empire
- Venice

LITERACY

Between 1400 and 1700 literacy, or the ability to read and write, increased in most of Europe. It was aided by changing attitudes toward education inspired by humanism and the ideals of religious leaders, as well as by the advent of the printing press.

The ability to read and write was always an important skill for people in certain professions and vocations, such as monks and nuns, priests, and notaries. In the late 15th century humanists such as Marsilio Ficino (1433–1499) and Pico della Mirandola (1463–1494) promoted the idea of the scholar–gentleman as the ideal of noble culture. They cultivated the idea that a person should use their free will to seek knowledge and to express themselves clearly, and that a good citizen should be educated and contribute to the public life of society.

HUMANIST EDUCATION
The influence of humanist ideas led to many schools being set up in Italian city-states for the study of language, literature, and the arts. Humanist education emphasized that mastering the classical writing style exemplified by the Roman statesman Cicero (106–143 B.C.) was a virtue in itself. The schools focused on the study of Latin and ancient Greek that nobody spoke in their day-to-day lives. Latin was used by the church, priests, and scholars, as well as for legal documents.

As governments became more complex, members of the educated upper classes entered the service of the state and used their skills as lawyers, doctors, advisers, and diplomats. In northern and eastern Europe, where monarchies ruled and the environment remained more rural, the nobles became attached to royal courts, and the use of Latin ensured that only a few could work at the highest levels.

Another kind of education was promoted in the merchant cities of Italy, southern France, Germany, the Low Countries, and England. Here, knowledge of Latin was of less use than having administrative and accountancy skills. In many cities, such as Florence,

A noblewoman looks up from reading a book in this 16th-century painting. Upper-class girls and women were taught to read and write, although few were educated to the same level as their male counterparts.

Genoa, Bruges, and London, the legal system began to move away from recording contracts and legal decisions in Latin. In these places members of the middle class focused on learning to read or write in the vernacular, or local language, of their area. Nevertheless, the ability to speak and write Latin remained for centuries the mark of a highly educated and cultured person.

SCHOOLS AND LEARNING

In the early modern era there were no public schools funded by cities or national governments. Tutors educated the nobility in their homes. Although both noble women and men learned to read and write, the subjects of study for women were more restricted. Women were encouraged to read poetry and religious texts, and to study those authors considered suitable for their roles as wives and mothers.

Middle-class people learned to read and write in the vernacular in schools set up by either the church or private scholars. Girls were less likely to learn to read than boys. Generally, these schools focused on the practical uses of reading, writing, and arithmetic: for example, their use in business. People considered that it took two years of attendance at school to learn to read but more than five years to be able to write. Many middle-class artisans invested in educating their children so that they could become city officials, clerks, and even notaries and lawyers.

NEW IMPETUS

The invention and rapid spread of the printing press from the middle of the 15th century contributed to the rise in literacy. Countless pamphlets and books were produced and circulated across Europe. The Bible was translated into German, English, French, and most other languages spoken in Europe.

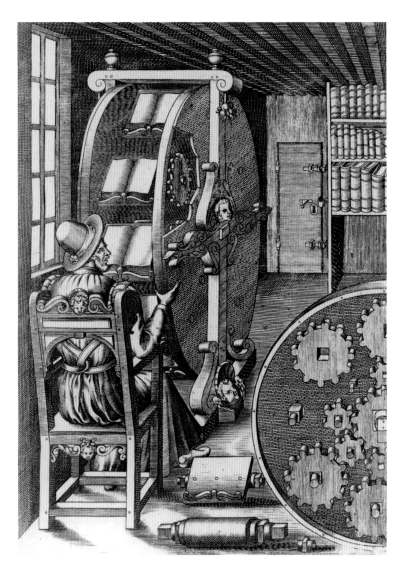

Religious figures also played a significant role in promoting literacy. Leading Protestant reformers such as Martin Luther (1483–1546) and John Calvin (1509–1564) stressed that education was a necessary duty of all Christians so that they could learn to read the Bible for themselves. As part of the Counter Reformation, the Catholic church promoted the education of young people in schools run by Dominicans and Jesuits.

In 1600 only one in four English adult males could read; by 1800 that number had doubled. Literacy in cities shot ahead of literacy in the rural areas, but nowhere in Europe during this period was literacy shrinking.

In this 16th-century print a man reads a book set in a machine that enables him to consult several volumes with ease.

SEE ALSO
- Academies
- Bibles and bible studies
- Books and libraries
- Humanism
- Language
- Printing
- Schools and schooling

LITERATURE

Literature reflects and responds to the state of the society in which it is created. In the 16th and 17th centuries humanist thought and the Reformation were two major influences for writers, but so too were the upheavals in society and behavior these movements brought about.

Humanism was already having a profound effect on literature by the beginning of the 1500s. The humanist movement had emerged in the previous century. It centered on admiration and study of ancient Greek and Roman (classical) thought and writing, and emphasized the potential and dignity of humankind.

FROM IMITATION TO SATIRE

With their admiration of all things classical, many humanist writers produced works that imitated or emulated the great writers of the past, such as the Roman historian Livy or the Greek philosopher Plato. For example, the Italian Jacopo Sannazaro's epic poem *The Motherhood of the Virgin* (1513) was very similar in style to the Roman poet Virgil's epic poem *Aeneid*.

Humanist writers also produced many radically new works, including satirical and didactic (instructional) writings, which attacked the foolishness of human behavior and offered moral alternatives. Among the most famous of these works are *In Praise of Folly* (1511) by the Dutch scholar Desiderius Erasmus (1466–1536) and *Utopia* (1516) by the English politician Thomas More. The central character of Erasmus's book is Dame Folly, who comments on human stupidity. Thomas More criticized contemporary society in a different way: He contrasted it with the fictional society of Utopia ("no

place"), a place in which people did not fear death, chose peace over war, and avoided displays of wealth.

Humanists were concerned with reading classical works in their original languages, as well as translating them into other languages. These activities led to a move away from Latin, which had been the dominant literary language of the medieval era, and a

A 19th-century illustration of the French poet Pierre de Ronsard addressing fellow members of the Pléiade, a group that promoted the use of French for literary works.

SPANISH PICARESQUE NOVELS

Spanish picaresque novels take their name from their central character, the *picaro*, a wretched, unfortunate figure who tries to make something of himself in the world, and in so doing allows the writer to satirize the values of contemporary society. Early examples of the picaresque novel include *Lazarillo de Tormes* (1554; author unknown) and *Guzmán de Alfarache* (1599) by Mateo Alemán. However, the best-known of all picaresque novels is *Don Quixote* (part one of which was published in 1605; part two in 1615) by Miguel de Cervantes. The story, with which Cervantes intended to parody the literary tradition of knightly romances, concerns the adventures of an easily deceived knight called Don Quixote and his down-to-earth squire Sancho Panza.

A title page from an English edition of Don Quixote *published in 1620. It shows Don Quixote and Sancho Panza on their travels.*

turn toward the use of vernacular (regional) languages in books. An early vernacular work was the epic *Judith* (1501), written in Croat by the scholar and poet Marko Marulic (1450–1524).

Historians regard vernacular books as the first step in a process that led to national literatures. By the end of the 1500s national literatures had evolved considerably. In Germany, for example, *volksbuchs*, gentle satires of small-town life, reinforced regional attitudes and identities. One *volksbuch* was *The Burghers of Schilda* (1598), in which the townsfolk of Schilda pretended to be stupid in the hope that other people would stop telling them what to do. However, their pretence was too good—they became genuinely stupid.

THE INFLUENCE OF RELIGION

The 16th and 17th centuries were times of enormous religious upheavals, and religion was a major influence on much of the period's literature. In one sense this influence was negative: Reeling from the effects of the Protestant Reformation, the Catholic church in Italy strongly discouraged the production of radical new works. The church placed any books that it considered contrary to its teachings on the Index of Prohibited Books. Consequently, by the later 16th century the intellectual and literary energy that had characterized Italy during the Renaissance had begun to stagnate.

In other ways the influence of religion on literature was positive. The Reformation inspired new translations of the Bible in a variety of languages. Many of these translations were literary masterpieces in their own right. In Spain a religious revival in the Catholic church stimulated a genre known as mystical literature, which concerned itself with the soul's ability to know God. The two best-known

A map illustration from an early edition of John Bunyan's religious allegory Pilgrim's Progress *(1678). The book is a symbolic account of a good man's journey through life. The map shows the course taken by Christian, the main character, from the City of Destruction to the Celestial City.*

mystical writers of the 16th century were Teresa of Avila (1515–1582) and John of the Cross (1542–1591). Another literary genre involved works that laid out religious beliefs or attacked those of another group. *Institutes of the Christian Religion* (1536) by the French Protestant John Calvin was one such work; for the Catholic side the French poet Pierre de Ronsard countered with his *Discourse on the Miseries of These Times* (1562).

BEGINNINGS OF THE NOVEL

One of the most important literary developments in the 15th and 16th centuries was the novel. Prose fiction first developed in countries such as France and the Netherlands in the mid-1400s, when, stimulated by the invention of the printing press, medieval epic poems were adapted, modernized, turned into prose and then

printed in large quantities. Another influence on the novel's development was the transition from reading aloud to reading to oneself, which encouraged more sophisticated narrative techniques to hold the reader's attention.

Early works of prose fiction include the French *Fierabras* (1478), a tale of adventure and chivalry involving the eighth-century King Charlemagne. However, it was with the Spanish picaresque novel that prose fiction began to reveal its true potential (*see box opposite*). The picaresque novel influenced later novels in the 17th century, including further parodies of epics, known as burlesques, and stories of quests, such as *Pilgrim's Progress* (1678) by the English preacher John Bunyan. In the 18th century the influence of the picaresque novel can be seen in the works of English novelists such as Thomas Fielding.

SEE ALSO

- Bibles and bible studies
- Books and libraries
- Drama
- Humanism
- Language
- Poetry
- Printing
- Shakespeare, William

LOCKE, JOHN

The English philosopher and political theorist John Locke (1632–1704) was one of the pioneers of modern thinking. He made substantial contributions to the study of politics, government, and philosophy, and his ideas were influential in prerevolutionary America.

John Locke was born in 1632 in the southwest of England. He studied medicine at Oxford University and was later appointed personal physician and confidential secretary to Lord Anthony Ashley Cooper, who became earl of Shaftesbury. Through Shaftesbury's influence Locke served in various government posts.

In 1675 Locke went to live in France, where he learned about the philosophy of René Descartes (1596–1650). He returned to England in 1679 but stayed for only a few years. Shaftesbury led attempts to exclude James, duke of York (later King James II), from the succession to the English throne. As a result, he fled to the Netherlands in 1682. Endangered by his association with Shaftesbury, Locke followed. He remained there until the overthrow of James II in 1688. A year later Locke returned to England as a member of the party escorting the princess of Orange, who was to be crowned Queen Mary II of England.

MAJOR WORKS

In 1690 Locke published his *Essay Concerning Human Understanding*, in which he examined the nature of human knowledge. He asserted that the main subject of philosophy should be the extent of the mind's ability to know. As such the essay was the principal statement of empiricism, a doctrine that aimed to reconcile traditional

philosophy with the scientific findings of Isaac Newton (1642–1727), whom Locke knew personally.

Among Locke's other work was an important book about politics. In *Two Treatises of Government* (1690) Locke concluded that the state exists to preserve the natural rights of its citizens; when it fails, the people have the right to rebel. The work had a profound influence on the subsequent history of England and its American colonies. John Locke died in 1704.

A portrait of John Locke, who is best known for his theories about government.

SEE ALSO

- Descartes, René
- Government, systems of
- Newton, Isaac
- Philosophy

LONDON

Long established as the largest city and the chief port of England, during the Reformation London consolidated its position as one of the great capitals of Europe. It thrived as a financial, commercial, and cultural center, even after devastating outbreaks of plague and fire.

London grew steadily between 1500 and 1700 both in area and population. In 1500 it had around 50,000 inhabitants. By 1700 this figure had risen to around 500,000, making the city bigger than Paris. London was made up of three distinct areas: the old Roman walled settlement known as the City, which was the center of trade, commerce, and finance; Westminster; the center of politics and government; and Southwark, on the south bank of the Thames River, which was a center of entertainment and recreation. London Bridge, which connected the City and Southwark, was London's only bridge until 1750.

The land between the City and Westminster was gradually built over, and by the early 17th century the term "London" covered all three areas, although they maintained separate municipal governments.

ROYAL RESIDENCES

In 1532 work began on two great royal residences in Westminster, which established London as the permanent seat of government in England. One was Saint James's Palace, an opulent complex of buildings that was later added to by Inigo Jones (1573–1652) and Christopher Wren (1632–1723), the outstanding architects of their day. Even more ambitious were the plans for Whitehall Palace, which Henry VIII wanted to replace the Tower of

London as the main royal residence. At first existing structures were remodeled, but in 1619 Inigo Jones began work on a new Banqueting House. Finished in 1622, the building was so magnificent that it inspired both Charles I and Charles II to commission an even larger palace, but the project was abandoned in 1698 after a fire.

COMMERCIAL CENTER

London grew rapidly as a center of trade between 1500 and 1700. In the mid-16th century England profited greatly from the collapse of Antwerp as a financial center. In the 1600s many London merchants had become rich from commercial ventures in Russia, the Levant (the lands of the eastern Mediterranean), India, and the English colony of Virginia.

This view of London in 1649 shows the Thames River with London Bridge in the center and the Tower of London at top right. This bustling built-up area was the commercial heart of London.

This painting of the Great Fire of London was made shortly after the event that ravaged the city between September 2 and 5, 1666. The picture shows roughly the same area as the illustration on p. 51. In the center the old Saint Paul's Cathedral is engulfed in flames.

During the reign of Elizabeth I (1558–1603) England's continuing growth as a commercial and military power was accompanied by London's development as a cultural center. As drama became a popular form of entertainment, playhouses sprang up in the capital. The earliest, named simply The Theatre, was erected in Shoreditch in 1576 by the actor James Burbage. By 1600 there were eight more, including The Globe in Southwark, where the plays of William Shakespeare (1564–1616) were first performed.

CIVIL WAR ALLEGIANCES

When the English Civil War broke out in 1642, some influential Londoners supported the Royalists. However, most were Puritans, and their support for Parliament was crucial in the defeat of King Charles I, who was executed in 1649. At the Restoration of the monarchy in 1660 Charles II secured the backing of London's citizens by promising them an amnesty, a new charter, and freedom of religion. During the Glorious Revolution of 1688 Londoners backed the Protestant William III in the overthrow of the Catholic king of England James II.

PLAGUE AND FIRE

Between the mid-16th and the mid-17th centuries the population of London increased from about 60,000 to 250,000. One in every 11 English people was a Londoner. Overcrowding was a serious problem. There was also a chronic lack of clean water and effective sanitation. In 1625 and 1665 there were outbreaks of plague, which spread rapidly and claimed more than 75,000 lives. Most buildings in the city were made of wood, and in 1666 the four-day Great Fire of London devastated the city, destroying more than 13,000 houses and nearly all the public buildings, including the original Saint Paul's Cathedral.

Right after the disaster Charles II used the revenue from a new coal tax to finance the reconstruction of London's buildings in brick and stone and the installation of sewers and pavements. Christopher Wren was one of the six architects appointed to run the project. He built more than 50 churches and a new Saint Paul's Cathedral, which was finished in 1711.

In 1694 the Bank of England was founded in the city, establishing London as the nation's financial center.

SEE ALSO

- Banks and banking
- Drama
- England
- Glorious Revolution
- Population
- Reformation
- Trade
- Urbanization

LOUIS XIV

Louis XIV, king of France from 1643 to 1715, reigned longer than any other monarch in the history of Europe; he is often seen as the archetype of an absolute ruler. During his reign he transformed France into the strongest power in Europe.

Louis XIV was born on September 5, 1638, and succeeded his father, Louis XIII, as king in 1643 at age four. While Louis was growing up, his mother Anne of Austria ruled as regent in his place, with the help of Cardinal Jules Mazarin. In 1648 the French nobility led an uprising, known as the Fronde, against Mazarin's efforts to centralize government. Mazarin suppressed the rebellion in 1653. From then on France steadily increased its power in Europe. In 1659 the Peace of the Pyrenees concluded a prolonged war between France and Spain. The treaty was sealed in 1660 when Louis XIV married Marie Thérèse, daughter of Philip IV, king of Spain.

LOUIS'S PATH TO THE THRONE
From an early age Louis planned to change the tradition in France whereby power resided with the monarch's advisers: At 17 he is reputed to have said, *"L'état, c'est moi"* (I am the state). When Mazarin died in 1661, Louis declared himself the absolute ruler of France. He believed in the divine right of kings and was certain that God had chosen him to rule France. For the rest of his life he controlled government

through his high state council and a number of ministers, including Jean-Baptiste Colbert, finance minister, and the Marquis de Louvois, head of the war department.

The early years of Louis's reign were a success. He effectively reformed both civil and criminal law. He also helped develop a more efficient tax system that raised money to subsidize French commerce and industry and to fund the development of France's overseas colonies, particularly in North America.

A portrait from 1667 showing Louis XIV surrounded by members of the Académie Royale des Sciences (the Royal Academy of Science). Louis's adviser, Jean-Baptiste Colbert, founded the academy in 1666.

Louis soon brought political stability in France; its economy flourished, and the country experienced a golden age.

FOREIGN AFFAIRS

In 1667 Louis claimed the Spanish Netherlands on behalf of his wife Marie Thérèse. In the resulting War of Devolution (1667–1668) Louis acquired important towns on France's eastern border in Flanders (now part of Belgium) and Hainault. Louis then entered the Anglo-Dutch War (1672–1678) on the side of the English; through the resulting Peace of Nijmegen (1678–1679) Louis acquired the province of Franche-Comté, extending France's border to the east. He then instituted a system called "courts of reunion," which aimed to bring under his control areas outside of France where French people lived. This led to the annexation of several towns along the border with Germany.

In 1685 Louis revoked the 1598 Edict of Nantes that had guaranteed the right of Huguenots (French Protestants) to their own form of worship. This led to an exodus of Huguenots. In response, in 1686 Protestant rulers in Europe formed an alliance against France called the League of Augsburg. In 1688 the Protestant king of England William III headed a broader coalition known as the Grand Alliance.

During the War of the Spanish Succession (1701–1714) Louis secured the Spanish throne for his grandson Philip V. In the Treaties of Utrecht (1713), which partly ended the war, Philip became king of Spain as long as France agreed not to merge with Spain.

FLOWERING CULTURE

During Louis's reign in France there was a great flowering of the arts, of which both he and Jean-Baptiste

Colbert were connoisseurs and patrons. He established and developed several academies, including those for painting and sculpture (1663), science (1666), architecture (1671), and music (1672). The literary Académie Française (1635) came under royal control in 1671.

Louis also oversaw a lavish building program that included the palace of the Louvre in Paris and the palace of Versailles just outside the city. Louis built Versailles as a showpiece. The palace and its magnificent gardens became the envy of Europe. The king moved his court there in 1682. In 1683 Louis XIV secretly married his mistress Madame de Maintenon, who strengthened his Catholic beliefs and encouraged piety in his court.

DEVOLUTION OF POWER

In 1693, after a long dispute with the pope, Louis abandoned his claims that the French church was independent of the Vatican. In one of his last acts Louis closed the Paris convents of the Jansenists, a Catholic dissident group who threatened the unity of the church. Louis died at the age of 77 on September 1, 1715.

This 17th-century painting shows Louis XIV, king of France, and his son the Dauphin, on horseback in the gardens of the palace of Versailles.

SEE ALSO
• Diplomacy
• France
• French Wars of Religion
• Huguenots
• Mazarin, Jules
• Monarchy and absolutism
• Reformation
• Versailles

LUTHER, MARTIN

Martin Luther (1483–1546) was the instigator of the Protestant Reformation in Germany and one of the most important theologians of his or any other era. His criticisms of the Catholic church drew him into a conflict that ultimately led to the formation of a new Christian church.

Luther was born in the town of Eisleben in the central German state of Saxony. His father was a miner but managed to pay for Luther to go to Erfurt University in 1501 to study law. Against his father's wishes in 1505 Luther entered the Augustinian monastery of Erfurt. He had vowed to Saint Anne that he would become a monk if she saved him from death during a violent thunderstorm.

CAREER AS A CLERIC

Luther was ordained a priest in 1507 and went on to become a lecturer at Wittenberg University in 1509, where he remained for the rest of his life. In 1511 he gained his theology doctorate.

Luther was, however, a man in a spiritual and emotional crisis. He was unsure that all the duties he performed as a monk brought him any closer to God and to salvation. He came to doubt the emphasis that the Catholic church placed on doing "good works" to gain salvation, believing that all people were born sinners, and that no actions could change this state. He found a solution in the New Testament letters of Paul, who asserted that "the just are saved by faith." Luther concluded that it was faith alone that saved. Good works were important, but they could not achieve salvation.

Luther's belief that *sola fide* ("faith alone") saved sinners drew him into a dispute with the Catholic church that

This portrait of Martin Luther by Lucas Cranach dates from around 1533. Luther's strong convictions, deep faith, and uncompromising personality were a driving force behind the Reformation.

led to his excommunication and eventually to the Protestant Reformation in Germany.

OBJECTIONS TO INDULGENCES

Luther strongly objected to the church's practice of selling indulgences, which people could buy to avoid punishment for past or future sins. On October 30, 1517, Luther nailed his Ninety-five Theses (arguments) against the sale of indulgences to the door of the Castle Church in Wittenberg. This was not an unusual act—at the time it was an accepted way of beginning a debate. It has since been taken to mark the start

LUTHER'S WORKS

Luther wrote extensively in his lifetime—academic works in Latin, closely argued explanations of his views in German, and simpler, propagandist works aimed at ordinary people. The years 1517 to 1522 were the high point of his productivity. During this period he made the first translation of the Bible in German. The newly invented printing presses turned out around 300,000 copies of his works. In 1520 he published three major works. One was *To the Christian Nobility of the German Nation*, which proposed that since the papacy had failed to preserve the true message of Christ, it was the responsibility of secular rulers to introduce and spread reforms. The second was *On the Babylonian Captivity of the Church*, which argued that the church had confused the message of the gospel by creating a complex system of priests and sacraments. The third was *The Liberty of the Christian*, which further developed these ideas.

The message of Luther's books was often clear from their titles. *Against the Murdering, Thieving Hordes of Peasants* was his response to the 1525 Peasants' Revolt in Germany, which he condemned. Another work, *Against the Papacy at Rome, Founded by the Devil*, reveals the extent to which Luther had turned against the Catholic church.

of the Reformation because of the train of events it set in motion. The archbishop of Mainz regarded Luther's theses as a challenge to his authority and alerted the pope. A local papal legate failed to make Luther retract his views. Luther was then summoned to a disputation (hearing) at Leipzig in 1519. Once again Luther refused to change his mind. He was also drawn into admitting that he believed that both the pope and a general council could make a mistake. In 1520 Luther published a series of books (*see box above*) putting forward his views. The pope excommunicated him. Support for his views began to grow.

In 1521 Holy Roman Emperor Charles V summoned Luther to the Diet (assembly) at Worms. Luther again refused to retract the views he had expressed in his books and was outlawed. Fearing for his life, he sought protection from Frederick the Wise, who, like many princes in Germany, was sympathetic to Luther's arguments.

Luther spent eight months in the safety of Wartburg Castle, where he had time to think through his ideas and work on biblical translations. In 1522 he was able to return to Wittenburg.

This engraving shows Luther preaching from the pulpit. Luther set out to reform the church, but his Ninety-five Theses on the inconsistencies of indulgences ended up dividing it permanently.

By this time Luther's ideas had become popular across Germany.

Luther's opposition to the 1525 Peasants' Revolt in Germany and his break with Erasmus and the humanists damaged his reputation. Divisions also appeared between Luther and other reformers, particularly Huldrych Zwingli (1484–1531). For the rest of his life Luther tried to resolve these divisions. In his later years Luther suffered from illness and depression. He died in his hometown in 1546.

SEE ALSO

- Catholic church
- Charles V
- France
- Germany
- Humanism
- Popular rebellions
- Reformation
- Zwingli, Huldrych

MAGELLAN, FERDINAND

The Portuguese mariner Ferdinand Magellan (about 1480–1521) was one of the most important explorers of the 16th century. He led the first expedition to sail across the newly discovered Pacific Ocean and right around the world, although he died before the voyage was complete.

Magellan was born into the Portuguese nobility. In 1505 he joined a voyage to India to break Muslim power, which was threatening Portuguese trade in the Indian Ocean. He later took part in fighting off the East African coast and in the Portuguese naval victory over the Arabs off Diu in the Indian Ocean in 1509. In 1512 Magellan was lamed while fighting in Morocco. After the king of Portugal refused his request for an increased pension, Magellan offered his services to King Charles I of Spain.

THE WESTERN PASSAGE

Under the Treaty of Tordesillas (1494) territories discovered in the Western Hemisphere belonged to Spain and those in the Eastern Hemisphere to Portugal. In 1513 the Spanish explorer Vasco Núñez de Balboa had sighted a new ocean on the far side of America. His discovery opened up the possibility of sailing westward to the Portuguese Spice Islands of the East Indies (the Moluccas), and laying claim to them as part of the western, Spanish, zone.

Magellan suggested such a voyage to King Charles, who approved his plan. Magellan's expedition left Seville on September 20, 1519. After months of searching, Magellan found a navigable

This 20th-century portrait celebrates Magellan and his achievements. It shows the explorer standing in front of his fleet of ships with sea charts at his side. The red cross of the Order of Santiago, a chivalric order with which the Spanish king invested Magellan, is displayed on the white cloth at left.

passage at the tip of South America, a treacherous strait later named for him. Sailing through this strait, he reached the new ocean: the Pacific. He then turned north up the coast of South America until, on December 18, 1520, he headed west into the unknown. He reached Guam on March 6, 1521, and from there sailed to the Philippines, where he was killed in a fight with natives on April 27, 1521. After Magellan's death Juan Sebastian del Cano took command of the expedition. He continued westward and returned to Spain on September 6, 1522.

SEE ALSO

• Colonization
• Exploration
• Navigation
• Ships
• Spanish Empire

MAGIC AND SUPERSTITION

In 1500 most Europeans believed in magic and superstition, but by 1700 many educated people had begun to cast aside such beliefs. However, the years between were marked by witch trials in which thousands of people were convicted and sentenced to death for practicing magic.

When the witch scare reached its height around 1600, King James VI of Scotland wrote of the "fearefull abounding ... of these detestable slaves of the Divel, the witches or enchanters." Some 20 years earlier the French philosopher Jean Bodin had written that sorcery was widespread and required strong punishment. However, many people did not share these negative views of witchcraft and magic. Magic was divided into several categories—black and white, low and high—and of these only black magic attracted widespread fear and loathing. People often accused witches of practicing black magic and thereby causing death and disease, bad weather, infertility, and damage to crops. However, people looked to white witches to counter black magic spells, as well as to cure illness, locate lost property, and predict the future.

Low magic (both black and white) was regarded as the preserve of uneducated village witches. High

A painting of a witches' coven made in 1607 by the Flemish artist Frans Francken II. It is packed with details associated with witchcraft and magic: the huge cauldron in the background, demons, ugly hags, skulls, and toads.

magic, in contrast, was practiced by people known as magi, who were regarded as highly educated and mystical figures. High magic derived from Neoplatonic philosophy, which was based on speculations about the writings of the ancient Greek philosopher Plato. It proposed that all parts of the universe are linked together: If a magus (singular of magi) performed the right actions, he or she (they were generally men) could harness the power of the universe. High magic was an occupation for educated people, usually of noble birth.

WITCHCRAFT ON TRIAL

The 16th and 17th centuries were notable for the large number of witch trials. It is estimated that they led to the execution of around 100,000 people, about 80 percent of whom were women. Entire communities were driven apart by accusations and counteraccusations of black magic.

The origins of the witch trials lay in a shift in religious and legal attitudes toward magic, from the 1400s on, that resulted in the belief that witches were in league with the Devil. In the Middle Ages the Catholic church had been very active in exposing and condemning heretics—people it believed had departed from the teachings of the church. Gradually, however, heresy and witchcraft became intermingled, since both heretics and witches were believed to have made a pact with the Devil. In addition, the Inquisition—a religious court set up to try heretics—provided a model for nonreligious courts to adopt in their trials of suspected witches. The *Malleus Maleficarum* (The Hammer of Witches), first published in 1486 by two Dominicans, Heinrich Kramer and James Sprenger, became a handbook for inquisitors, describing the heretical

WITCH PANICS

One of the worst aspects of the witch hunt was the way communities could become gripped with panic as people began to suspect and then accuse one another of being witches. Prosecutors often used torture to induce suspected witches to reveal their accomplices as well as their guilt—victims often accused others simply to end the pain. One example of a witch panic gripped the city of Ellwangen in southwest Germany between 1611 and 1612. It began when a 70-year-old woman confessed to witchcraft after being tortured. In the belief that the woman was part of a conspiracy of witches, other people were tortured; they in turn confessed and accused others. In all, 260 residents were executed. One of the most famous witch panics broke out in Salem, Massachusetts, in 1692. The panic led to the deaths of 19 people. Fortunately, panics such as Salem's were rare.

A witness gives evidence at one of the Salem witch trials in 1692.

behavior of witches and outlining ways to torture them.

Witchcraft prosecutions differed from country to country. In Germany and Austria the number of trials reached a peak between the 1580s and mid-1600s, and in Poland between 1675 and 1720. There were fewer trials in France, although a notable aspect of French trials was the number of people accused of bewitching convents. Witch trials were much less common in Italy,

Spain, Ireland, the Netherlands, and Scandinavia. However, there were many in England and Scotland. English trials generally differed in emphasis from those in other countries: The charge laid against witches had more to do with the black magic they had performed than with whether or not they had made a pact with the Devil. In Scotland witches were pursued with great ferocity—in contrast to England, the charge of being in league with the "Great Enemy" (the Devil) was central to Scottish prosecutions.

ASTROLOGY

Astrologers were not persecuted in the 16th and 17th centuries, partly because many astrologers were educated people, in contrast to the majority of accused witches, who came from the poorer, uneducated classes. Another reason was the mainstream acceptance of astrology in European society.

In the early 1500s astrology formed part of an educated person's outlook on

This illustration of two astrologers under a planetary tree, a symbol linking the known planets in the universe, is from a 17th-century edition of a book by the German alchemist Basil Valentine. The picture reflects the belief that astrologers could forecast earthly and human events using the stars, sun, and moon.

life and the universe. People considered knowledge of the subject necessary to understand how the mind and body worked. For example, doctors often used astrological diagrams in which each part of the human body was linked to a planet, star, or sign of the Zodiac to diagnose diseases.

Astrology centered around the belief that the movements of the stars and planets influenced life on earth. Astrologers analyzed charts of the position of the stars and planets, and used them to predict future events.

Astrological predictions were based on the view that the planets revolved around the earth they influenced. This view was proved to be wrong in the 17th century when the sun rather than the earth was shown to be the center of the universe.

Rulers often consulted astrologers. In 1558 the English astrologer John Dee was asked to name a lucky day for the coronation of Queen Elizabeth I. In 1669 the French King Louis XIV chose an astrologer to be France's diplomat at the court of Charles II after Louis discovered the English king's fondness for the subject—however, when the French astrologer failed to select any winners for Charles at a horse race, he was sent back to France in disgrace.

Astrology was also popular with ordinary people, as can be seen from the huge demand for almanacs. They were similar to pocket diaries but included tables showing the position of the stars and the planets, as well as astrological forecasts for upcoming events. In 17th-century England sales of almanacs exceeded those of bibles.

THE DECLINE OF MAGIC

Between 1600 and 1700 there was a marked decline in the number of educated people who believed in magic and astrology, as well as auspicious days (*see box below*), ghosts, fairies, omens, and charms. Some historians propose that the reason for this change lay in the scientific revolution of the 1600s: As philosophers and scientists such as Galileo, Isaac Newton, and Johannes Kepler published their theories, the supernatural worldview came to have less meaning. Other historians suggest that the scientific revolution was itself the product of a deeper change in attitudes, and that it was this change that resulted in the decline of magic.

NEW ATTITUDES

The change in attitudes was from a medieval outlook that regarded humans as helpless souls, adrift in a hostile world and capable of being saved only by God, to a more optimistic one in which individuals controlled their own destinies. Humanism contributed to this shift, as did both the Reformation and the Counter Reformation.

Developments in science were one outcome of changing attitudes; others included new technologies, a new approach to trade, and exploration of the unknown parts of the world. Yet

while educated people began to reassess their opinion of magic and superstition, it would be some time before ordinary people came to share their skepticism. However, by the end of the 17th century magic and astrology were on their way to the margins of human belief and experience.

A painting of an astronomer by the Dutch artist Gerard Dou in around 1650. Early astronomers were often also astrologers.

LUCKY AND UNLUCKY DAYS

One widely held superstition was that there were days when it was good to perform a certain act and days when doing so was considered to be inviting misfortune. More often than not, people did not know why they considered one day to be better than another for marriage, or travel, or even having a haircut—it was simply a generally accepted view. One reason for the belief, however, can be found in the medieval Catholic church, which, while it condemned the notion of unlucky and lucky

times, unwittingly reinforced it by promoting saints' days, such as Saint Stephen's Day and Saint James's Day. The church encouraged the notion that such days were special by teaching that to commit a sin on one of them was far worse than committing it on any other day. Protestants were quick to accuse Catholics of encouraging superstitions. Protestants, in contrast, opposed the idea of saints' days. For them, the only special time was the Sabbath, the day of rest.

SEE ALSO

- Astronomy
- Counter Reformation
- Crime and punishment
- Heresy and heretics
- Humanism
- Inquisition
- Reformation
- Science
- Scotland

MAMLUKS, DEFEAT OF THE

The Mamluks dominated Egypt and Syria for almost 300 years until they were beaten in battle by the Ottomans in 1517. Defeat brought an end to their sultanate, but the old ruling class survived more or less intact and retained considerable influence, particularly in Egypt.

The term "Mamluk" means "slave." The Mamluks were originally slaves of the caliphs, the rulers of the Islamic Empire. From the ninth century the caliphs created slave armies that eventually rebelled against them. From 1250, when a Mamluk army overthrew the Ayyubid Dynasty, a line of 50 Mamluk sultans governed Egypt and Syria.

The Turkish Bahri Mamluks ruled until 1382 and were succeeded by the Circassian Burji Mamluks, from the northern Caucasus, who ruled until 1517. Mamluk rule was not hereditary. Instead, leading Mamluks fought each other to gain the sultanate. In 1260 the Mamluks, led by Baybars, defeated the Mongols at the Battle of Ayn Jalut in Palestine, forcing them back to Persia. This victory established the Mamluks as a major power.

For many years the Mamluks grew rich from taxing trade goods that passed overland through Egypt between Europe and the Indian Ocean. By the end of the 15th century they had raised their tariffs too high, and foreign merchants had begun to seek new routes that avoided Mamluk lands. In 1497 Portuguese explorers opened a direct sea route between Europe and Asia via the Cape of Good Hope,

bypassing Egypt. At about the same time, Syrian merchants began to detour around Egypt, using the overland route through Aleppo to Iraq.

A PERIOD OF CRISES
The resulting economic recession left the Mamluks ill-equipped to cope with the series of natural disasters that befell them at the start of the 1500s. Egypt

The Mamluks—shown here storming a citadel—were originally slave soldiers who had converted to Islam.

fell victim to plague, drought, and famine in quick succession. The government had become corrupt and did not provide an adequate response to the crises, and Egypt went into decline.

For the neighboring Ottoman sultanate the decline of Egypt presented an opportunity to seize the agricultural lands along the banks of the Nile River, one of the most fertile regions in the world. Between 1485 and 1490 the two sultanates fought a few mainly inconclusive battles. However, the Ottomans developed handguns and cannons that gave them an overwhelming advantage on the battlefield. The Mamluks did not use these new weapons, preferring to rely on their skilled cavalry using swords and shields. They were no match for the Ottoman artillery and infantry. As a result, the decisive war of 1516–1517 was quick and one-sided: After the fighting ended, the Ottomans under Selim I (ruled 1512–1520) entered Cairo and from there dominated all the former Mamluk territories of Egypt, Syria, and western Arabia.

EGYPT UNDER THE OTTOMANS

Once Selim had subjugated Egypt, he offered to preserve the existing Mamluk administration as long as it accepted vassal status. When the sultan refused, Selim had him executed and appointed an Ottoman pasha (governor) to run the country. However, he still left Mamluk governors in charge of the 12 sanjaks, or provinces, of Egypt.

Over the next century the balance of power swung between the Ottoman pashas and the Mamluk aristocracy. Whenever the Mamluks appeared to be gaining too much strength, the Ottoman sultan would respond by ordering a clampdown.

Thus, despite their defeat in 1517 the Mamluks were substantially

unaffected by Ottoman rule. The worst change was that while previously they had extorted more or less whatever they wanted from ordinary Egyptians, they now had to compete for the spoils with Ottoman administrators. The Mamluks were still appointed to government offices, and eventually they were able to dominate the Ottoman ruling class.

Although the practice of passing official posts from father to son had been banned under Mamluk rule, the Ottomans allowed it. This system weakened the conquerors' position because loyalty to the state was undermined by the competing claims of family. Over the following two centuries the Mamluks formed dynastic "houses" within a wide range of occupations and professions.

For a while the Ottomans were able to take advantage of the feuds that sprang up between families vying to extend their power. However, by the end of the 17th century the Mamluks had regained effective control of the army, as well as of the country's finances and the government. In return for annual payments the Ottomans were now forced to recognize the independence of the Mamluks.

This fortress in Alexandria, Egypt, was an important defensive stronghold for the Mamluks. It was built by Sultan Qait Bay, who was involved in military clashes with the Ottoman Turks from the mid-1480s.

SEE ALSO

• Islam
• Ottoman Empire
• Persian–Ottoman wars

MANNERISM

Mannerism was an artistic style that spread from Italy to much of Europe in the mid-1500s. The work of mannerist artists is characterized by an obsession with style and with creating elegant and refined works of art, as well as with experimenting with traditional forms.

Literature was the first art form to develop a mannerist style, particularly in courtly literature addressed to aristocrats. The Italian word *maniera* (style), from which the term mannerism derives, came from the French word *manière*, which appeared in French courtly literature in the 1200s and denoted sophisticated behavior. In the early 1500s a literary movement based in Rome became renowned for its obsession with style.

This movement was led by writers such as Pietro Bembo, who argued that the style and language of a work were more important than its content.

CHARACTERISTICS

Mannerist writers and artists saw themselves as continuing the revival of the classical tradition of ancient Greek and Roman values that had begun in the Italian Renaissance. However, unlike High Renaissance art, which was

THE PALAZZO DEL TÈ

This photo shows one of the painted walls in the Room of Giants.

The Palazzo del Tè in Mantua, Italy, is one of the finest examples of mannerist architecture. It was designed by Giulio Romano and built between the mid-1520s and the mid-1530s. The palazzo (palace) was intended for festivities and not as a place of residence. It is a single-story building situated around a courtyard. Romano used features such as columns and decorative elements based on classical architecture. However, he deliberately arranged them in unusual ways in order to shock and surprise the onlooker. Inside, the palazzo contains a series of differently shaped rooms, with elaborately decorated walls, ceilings, and mosaic floors. Its most famous room is the Room of Giants, which depicts the mythological war between the gods of Olympus and the Titans.

characterized by balance, order, and idealized representations of human figures and nature, mannerist art was often exaggerated, containing sharply contrasting features or bizarre out-of-place elements.

Mannerist artists such as Giulio Romano (about 1499–1546) portrayed humans with overly muscular bodies. Other artists depicted figures with strangely shaped limbs and heads, such as Parmigianino (1503–1540) in his *Madonna with the Long Neck* (1535). However, distorted human figures were only one aspect of mannerist art. Other features included experimenting with space and scale, the relationship of objects to each other, and the use of color. The inspiration for this experimentation lay in the 16th-century admiration of virtuosity—the ability to be inventive and solve difficult problems without suggesting any effort or strain whatsoever.

SCULPTURE AND BUILDINGS

Mannerism found expression in all forms of art in the 16th century. Giambologna (1529–1608) was perhaps the most important mannerist sculptor. Working in Italy, he portrayed figures in complex but elegant and graceful poses, such as his *Mercury* (1570–1580). Complexity and stylishness were features of mannerist architecture, too. Examples include the Villa Farnesina, built in Rome for the powerful Farnese family by Baldassare Peruzzi (1481–1536), and the Palazzo del Tè in Mantua (*see box opposite*). At first sight, the Villa Farnesina's main room appears to be walled on only three sides, the fourth side opening onto a view of Rome. This view, however, is a conceit, or trick, of the kind enjoyed by mannerist artists: The city scene, as well as the columns around it and the garden in the foreground, are painted.

RISE AND FALL

Mannerism developed in Italy in the 1520s and soon spread to other parts of Europe. The invention of printing aided its spread. Artists could easily obtain prints of mannerist works of art and decorative motifs, which they could copy in their own work. The style was also spread by Italian artists working abroad, particularly after the sack of Rome (1527), and by foreign artists who visited Italy. Mannerism remained fashionable in parts of Europe until the 1590s, when a new approach known as the baroque became popular.

Rosso Fiorentino's **Deposition from the Cross** *(1521). Its unnatural colors and distorted scale are typical of mannerism.*

SEE ALSO

- Architecture
- Baroque
- Painting
- Renaissance
- Sculpture

MANUFACTURING

From 1500 the largely rural way of life of many Europeans changed. As trade grew, workers sought better-paid jobs in cities, and businessmen looked for cheaper ways to produce goods. The system they came up with, manufacturing, took industry back to the countryside.

The word *manufacture* literally means to make things by hand. Before the 1500s Europeans relied on skilled artisans or their own labor to provide the necessities of life such as clothes, shoes, tools, pottery, and weapons. Craftspeople working under a master craftsperson in workshops often made a product from beginning to end. For example, women would buy wool and spin it into thread, which they then wove themselves to form rough woolen cloth to make clothing. These steps were usually all completed either by one family or a couple of families working together. In the late Middle Ages this system began to change, as guilds emerged to regulate work and quality. A peasant family might still spin and weave for their own needs; but if they wanted to sell their wool or the cloth it was made into, they had to use the guild system.

GETTING AROUND THE GUILDS
By the 1500s guilds were so strong that they regulated every step of cloth manufacturing, with some members being paid to spin, others to dye, and yet others to weave. Each person could do only his or her job at the price set by the guild. Some businessmen saw this system as a waste of resources. They began to find ways around guilds in order to manufacture cheaper goods. Since guilds mainly held power in or near towns, entrepreneurs began to take raw materials to the countryside, where the guilds did not control the workforce. There they started the so-called "putting-out system." The investor, or entrepreneur, would buy wool and distribute it, or put it out, to several peasant households in the countryside. There the wool would be carded—combed and cleaned—and spun. The investor would then pay the family on the basis of how much wool was processed and transport the yarn to other households where it would be woven into cloth. The next stage was

Women Weaving *by Italian artist Francesco Bassano (1549–1592). Weaving was one of the final steps in the manufacture of cloth. The weaving industry in Italy thrived during the 16th and 17th centuries.*

MANUFACTURING BOOKS

While the guilds lost power in textiles and other industries between 1500 and 1700, they remained strong in some trades that flourished in an urban environment. Printing is one of the best examples. There were nearly 1,000 printing presses in operation across Europe in 250 towns by 1500. They were hand-built, and their movable type was forged by metalworkers mainly located in cities. The presses employed typesetters who laid out the text of each page of a pamphlet or book to be printed and boys and men who inked the type and worked the press. The industry became so important that between 1500 and 1600 around 40,000 editions were produced in Lyons and Paris alone. The scribes' guild attempted to block the advent of the printing press in order to protect their own jobs of hand-copying letters and texts. But soon they either joined with printers or were forced out of their jobs as the new technology created a new class of workers and skills.

to collect the cloth for bleaching and dyeing; finally the cloth would be taken and distributed for sale. The putting-out system worked most effectively for the textile industry, but it was developed for other goods as well.

EUROPEAN MANUFACTURING

Different areas of Europe specialized in the manufacture of goods based on the raw materials available. Belgium was a producer of woolens, Italy of silk and woolens, Germany of clocks, toys, and woodwork products, England of iron and textiles, and France of metalwork.

One advantage of the system to rural workers was that it allowed them to supplement their income from farming. In busy plowing and harvesting seasons the whole family might work in the fields. In winter or between harvests, however, the family could work in a different industry, for example, manufacturing cloth. Young children were given easy tasks such as carding wool, fetching wood for the fire, or sweeping away wood shavings. Older children learned to spin, weave, or carve, while adults did most of the more difficult finishing work.

SEE ALSO

- Books and libraries
- Clocks and calendars
- Daily life
- Guilds and crafts
- Inventions and inventors
- Technology
- Textiles

TIMELINE

♦ **1492** Christopher Columbus lands in the Bahamas, claiming the territory for Spain.

♦ **1494** Charles VIII of France invades Italy, beginning four decades of Italian wars.

♦ **1494** The Treaty of Tordesillas divides the "new world" between Spain and Portugal.

♦ **1498** Portuguese navigator Vasco da Gama sails around Africa to reach Calicut, India.

♦ **1509** Dutch humanist scholar Desiderius Erasmus publishes *In Praise of Folly*, a satire on religion and society.

♦ **1511** The Portuguese capture Melaka in Southeast Asia.

♦ **1515** Francis I of France invades Italy, capturing Milan.

♦ **1516** Charles, grandson of Holy Roman emperor Maximilian I, inherits the Spanish throne as Charles I.

♦ **1517** The German monk Martin Luther nails his Ninety-five Theses to a church door in Wittenberg, Germany, setting the Reformation in motion.

♦ **1518** The Portuguese begin trading in slaves from Africa.

♦ **1519** Charles I of Spain is elected Holy Roman emperor as Charles V.

♦ **1519–1521** Spanish conquistador Hernán Cortés conquers Mexico for Spain.

♦ **1520** Suleyman the Magnificent becomes sultan of the Ottoman Empire.

♦ **1520** Portuguese navigator Ferdinand Magellan rounds the tip of South America and is the first European to sight the Pacific Ocean.

♦ **1521** Pope Leo X excommunicates Martin Luther.

♦ **1521** At the Diet of Worms, Luther refuses to recant his views. The Holy Roman emperor outlaws him.

♦ **1522** One of Magellan's ships completes the first circumnavigation of the globe.

♦ **1523** Gustav Vasa becomes king of Sweden and dissolves the Kalmar Union that had dominated Scandinavia.

♦ **1523–1525** Huldrych Zwingli sets up a reformed church in Zurich, Switzerland.

♦ **1525** Holy Roman Emperor Charles V defeats and captures Francis I of France at the Battle of Pavia.

♦ **1525** In Germany the Peasants' Revolt is crushed; its leaders, including the radical Thomas Münzer, are executed.

♦ **1525** William Tyndale translates the New Testament into English.

♦ **1526** Mongol leader Babur invades northern India and establishes the Mogul Empire.

♦ **1526** At the Diet of Speyer German princes are granted the authority to allow Lutheran teachings and worship in their own territories.

♦ **1526** Suleyman the Magnificent defeats Hungarian forces at the Battle of Mohács.

♦ **1527** Charles V's forces overrun Italy and sack Rome.

♦ **1529** In the Peace of Cambrai with Charles V, Francis I of France renounces all French claims in Italy temporarily confirming Spanish supremacy.

♦ **1529** The Ottoman sultan Suleyman the Magnificent besieges the city of Vienna.

♦ **1531** German Protestant princes form the Schmalkaldic League to defend themselves.

♦ **1531–1532** Spanish conquistador Francisco Pizarro conquers Peru for Spain by defeating the Inca Empire.

♦ **1532** Niccolò Machiavelli's *The Prince* is published.

♦ **1534** The earl of Kildare, Thomas Lord Offaly, leads a revolt against Henry VIII's rule in Ireland.

♦ **1534** Henry VIII of England breaks away from the authority of the pope and establishes the Church of England.

♦ **1534** Martin Luther publishes his German translation of the New Testament.

♦ **1535–1536** The city of Geneva adopts Protestantism and expels all Catholic clergy.

♦ **1536** Henry VIII orders the dissolution of the monasteries.

♦ **1536** John Calvin publishes his *Institutes of the Christian Religion*, which sets out central Protestant principles.

♦ **1539** Ignatius Loyola founds the Society of Jesus (Jesuits).

♦ **1541** John Calvin sets up a model Christian community in Geneva, Switzerland.

♦ **1542** Pope Paul III reestablishes the Inquisition, a medieval religious court designed to combat heresy.

♦ **1543** The Flemish anatomist Andreas Vesalius publishes his handbook of anatomy *On the Structure of the Human Body*.

♦ **1543** Polish astronomer Nicolaus Copernicus publishes *On the Revolutions of the Heavenly Orbs*, which challenged contemporary beliefs by describing a sun-centered universe.

♦ **1545** Pope Paul III organizes the Council of Trent to counter the threat of Protestantism and reinvigorate the church.

♦ **1547** Ivan IV (the Terrible) becomes czar of Russia.

♦ **1547** Charles V defeats the Schmalkaldic League at the Battle of Mühlberg.

♦ **1553** Mary I restores the Catholic church in England.

♦ **1555** In the Peace of Augsburg Charles V allows German princes to decide the religion in their territories.

♦ **1555** Charles V abdicates, dividing his vast lands between his brother Ferdinand and son Philip.

♦ **1558** On the death of Mary I, her half-sister Elizabeth I becomes queen of England.

♦ **1559** Elizabeth I restores the Church of England.

♦ **1559** Pope Paul IV institutes the Index of Prohibited Books.

♦ **1562** The Wars of Religion break out in France.

♦ **1563** The Council of Trent ends having clarified Catholic doctrine and laid the basis of the Counter Reformation.

♦ **1566** The Dutch begin a revolt against Spanish rule.

♦ **1569** Flemish cartographer Gerardus Mercator publishes a world map using a new method of projection.

♦ **1571** Philip II of Spain leads an allied European force to victory over the Ottomans at the naval Battle of Lepanto.

♦ **1572** French Catholics murder thousands of Protestants across France in the Saint Bartholomew's Day Massacre.

♦ **1579** Seven Dutch provinces form the Union of Utrecht to fight for independence from Spanish rule.

♦ **1582** The warlord Toyotomi Hideyoshi becomes effective ruler of Japan.

♦ **1588** Philip II launches the Armada invasion fleet against England, but it is destroyed.

♦ **1590** Toyotomi Hideyoshi expels Christian missionaries from Japan.

♦ **1593** The English playwright William Shakespeare publishes his first work, *Venus and Adonis* beginning his prolific and successful career in the theater.

♦ **1598** The Persian Safavid ruler Shah Abbas the Great moves his capital to Esfahan.

♦ **1598** In the Edict of Nantes Henry IV of France grants Huguenots considerable rights, bringing an end to the French Wars of Religion.

♦ **1600** The English East India Company is founded in London to control trade with India and East Asia.

♦ **1602** The Dutch government establishes the Dutch East India Company.

♦ **1603** In Japan Tokugawa Ieyasu unites the country under his rule as shogun, ushering in a age of peace and prosperity.

♦ **1603** James VI of Scotland also becomes king of England as James I on the death of Elizabeth I.

♦ **1605** The Gunpowder Plot: A group of Catholics including Guy Fawkes fail to blow up the English Parliament.

♦ **1607** Henry Hudson sails to the Barents Sea in search of a northeastern passage to Asia.

♦ **1607** John Smith founds the English colony of Jamestown in Virginia.

♦ **1611** James I's authorized Bible, the King James Version, is published.

♦ **1616** Cardinal Richelieu becomes the prime minister of France.

♦ **1618** The Defenestration of Prague marks the beginning of the Thirty Years' War.

♦ **1620** The *Mayflower* pilgrims found the colony of New Plymouth in Massachusetts.

♦ **1621** Huguenots (French Protestants) rebel against King Louis XIII of France.

♦ **1625** Charles I is crowned king of England.

♦ **1629** Charles I dissolves Parliament and rules independently until 1640.

♦ **1631** The Mogul Emperor Shah Jahan builds the Taj Mahal as a mausoleum for his wife Mumtaz.

♦ **1632** Galileo Galilei publishes his *Dialogue Concerning the Two Chief World Systems,* in which he supports Copernicus's views of a sun-centered universe.

♦ **1633** Galileo is tried for heresy and sentenced to house arrest by the Roman Inquisition.

♦ **1637–1638** After a rebellion led by Christians in Japan 37,000 Japanese Christians are executed and many Europeans expelled from the country.

♦ **1640** Portuguese peasants rebel against Spanish rule and declare John of Braganza their king. Portugal finally regains its independence in 1668.

♦ **1641** French philosopher René Descartes publishes one of his most important works, *Meditations on First Philosophy*.

♦ **1642** Civil war breaks out in England between the king and Parliament.

♦ **1642** Jules Mazarin follows Cardinal Richelieu to become prime minister of France.

♦ **1643** Louis XIV becomes king of France. During his reign France becomes powerful.

♦ **1648** The Thirty Years' War comes to an end with the Treaty of Westphalia.

♦ **1648–1653** The Fronde, a series of civil wars, breaks out in France.

♦ **1649** The English king Charles I is executed and England becomes a republic.

♦ **1652** England and the Dutch Republic clash in the first Anglo-Dutch Naval War.

♦ **1653** The English Puritan Oliver Cromwell dissolves Parliament and rules England as lord protector.

♦ **1660** The English Parliament restores Charles II as king.

♦ **1660** The Royal Society of London is founded to promote scientific enquiry.

♦ **1661** Louis XIV begins work on the palace of Versailles outside Paris.

♦ **1661** Manchu Emperor Kang-hsi comes to power in China. His long reign marks a golden age in Chinese history.

♦ **1665** The Great Plague in London kills around a thousand people every week.

♦ **1666** French minister Jean-Baptiste Colbert establishes the French Academy to promote the sciences.

♦ **1666** The Great Fire of London destroys a large part of the English capital.

♦ **1670** The English Hudson's Bay Company is founded to occupy lands and trade in North America.

♦ **1678** English Puritan writer John Bunyan publishes his hugely popular allegorical book *Pilgrim's Progress.*

♦ **1683** The Turkish Ottoman army besieges Vienna for the second time.

♦ **1685** Louis XIV revokes the Edict of Nantes, depriving French Protestants of all religious and civil liberties. Hundreds of thousands of Huguenots flee France.

♦ **1688** In the Glorious Revolution the Protestant Dutch leader, William of Orange, is invited to replace James II as king of England.

♦ **1689** The Bill of Rights establishes a constitutional monarchy in England. William III and his wife Mary II jointly rule England and Scotland.

♦ **1694** The Bank of England is founded in London.

♦ **1699** Turks withdraw from Austria and Hungary.

♦ **1700–1721** The Great Northern War between Sweden and Russia and its allies weakens Swedish power.

♦ **1701** The War of the Spanish Succession breaks out over the vacant Spanish throne.

♦ **1704** Isaac Newton publishes his book *Optics* on the theory of light and color.

♦ **1707** The Act of Union unites England and Scotland. The seat of Scottish government is moved to London.

♦ **1712** Peter the Great makes Saint Petersburg the new capital of Russia, beginning a period of westernization.

♦ **1713–1714** The treaties of Utrecht are signed by England and France, ending the War of the Spanish Succession.

♦ **1715** The sun king King Louis XIV of France dies, marking the end of a golden age in French culture.

GLOSSARY

Absolutism
A system of government in which far-reaching power is held by a monarch or ruler over his or her subjects.

Alchemy
A tradition of investigative thought that tried to explain the relationship between humanity and the universe and exploit it, for example, by finding a way to turn base metal into gold.

Baroque
An artistic style originating in the 17th century characterized by dramatic effects and ornamentation, which aimed to evoke a strong emotional response.

Calvinists
Followers of the French Protestant reformer John Calvin. Calvinism emphasized the sovereignty of God and predestination—the idea that that God decided in advance who would gain eternal life.

Counter Reformation
The Catholic church's efforts to reinvigorate itself, bring an end to abuses, clarify its teachings, and prevent the spread of Protestantism.

Diet
An assembly of the rulers of the Holy Roman Empire, who gathered to pass laws and make important decisions.

Doctrine
A specific principle or belief, or system of beliefs, taught by a religious faith.

Elector
A leading landowner in the Holy Roman Empire who had a vote in the election of the Holy Roman emperor.

Enclosure
A process by which major landowners extended their holdings across common land.

Excommunication
A punishment in which a person was banned from taking part in the rites of the Catholic church.

Franciscans
Members of a Catholic religious order founded in the early 13th century by Saint Francis of Assisi.

Guild
An association of merchants, professionals, or craftsmen organized to protect the interests of its members and to regulate the quality and cost of their services.

Heresy
A belief that is contrary to the teachings of a religious faith.

Huguenots
The name given to Calvinists in France.

Humanism
An academic approach based on the study of "humanities"—that is, ancient Greek and Roman texts, history, and philosophy—which stressed the importance of developing rounded, cultured individuals.

Iconoclasm
The destruction of religious objects, usually by those who disapproved of the use of images in worship.

Indulgences
The cancelation or reduction of punishments for sins granted by the Catholic church in return for good works or money.

Inquisition
A powerful medieval religious court that was revived by the Catholic church in the 16th century to stamp out ideas contrary to Catholic teachings.

Janissaries
Members of an elite infantry corps in the Ottoman army.

Jesuits
Members of a Catholic order founded in the 16th century by Ignatius Loyola. They were famous for their work as educators and missionaries.

Laity or laypeople
Members of a religious faith who are not clergy.

Lutherans
Followers of the German Protestant reformer Martin Luther. He protested against abuses in the Catholic church and argued that the scriptures, not church traditions, were the ultimate religious authority.

Mass or Eucharist
A key Christian sacrament of thanksgiving for the sacrifice of Jesus's life celebrated with wine and bread representing his body and blood.

Mercantilism
An economic system under which a government regulated manufacturing and trade in the belief that high exports and low imports would enrich the country's treasury and make the state powerful.

Mercenary
A soldier who fights for any employer in return for wages.

Papacy
The pope and his advisers in Rome who govern the Catholic church.

Patriarch
The title given to Orthodox church leaders: The most important patriarchs were the bishops of Antioch, Rome, Alexandria, Constantinople, and Jerusalem.

Patron
Someone who orders and pays for a work of art or supports, usually financially, the work of an artist or thinker.

Protestant
Someone who follows one of the Christian churches set up during the Reformation in reaction to the corruption of the Catholic church.

Sacrament
An important Christian ritual, or ceremony, such as Mass or baptism. The number and nature of the sacraments were issues of major debate during the Reformation.

Secular
A term to describe something nonreligious as opposed to something religious.

Theology
The study of religion.

Tithe
A tax of one-tenth of a person's annual produce or income payable to the church.

Usury
The practice of making a dishonest profit, such as charging high interest on a loan, which was considered sinful by the medieval church.

Vernacular
The everyday language spoken by the people of a country or region, rather than a literary or formal language such as Latin.

FURTHER READING

Barry, J., M. Hester, and G. Roberts (eds.). *Witchcraft in Early Modern Europe: Studies in Culture and Belief.* New York: Cambridge University Press, 1996.

Black, C. F. *Church, Religion, and Society in Early Modern Italy.* New York: Palgrave, 2001.

Boorstin, Daniel J. *The Discoverers.* New York: Harry N. Abrams, 1991.

Collinson, Patrick. *The Reformation: A History.* New York: Modern Library, 2004.

Darby, G. (ed.). *The Origins and Development of the Dutch Revolt.* New York: Routledge, 2001.

Dixon, C. S. *The Reformation in Germany.* Malden, Mass.: Blackwell Publishers, 2002.

Duffy, Eamon. *Saints and Sinners: A History of the Popes.* New Haven, Conn.: Yale University Press, 1997.

Elliott , J. H. *Europe Divided 1559–1598.* Second edition, Malden, Mass.: Blackwell Publishers, 2000.

Gäbler, U., and R.C.L. Gritsch (trans.). *Huldrych Zwingli: His Life and Work.* Philadelphia: Fortress Press, 1998.

Goodwin, Jason. *Lords of the Horizons: A History of the Ottoman Empire.* New York: Henry Holt, 1999.

Henry, J. *The Scientific Revolution and the Origins of Modern Science.* Second edition, New York: Palgrave, 2001.

Jaffer, Amin, and Anna Jackson (eds.). *Encounters: The Meeting of Asia and Europe 1500–1800.* New York: Harry N. Abrams, 2004.

Jewell, Helen M. *Education in Early Modern England.* New York: St. Martin's Press, 1998.

Jones, M. D. W. *The Counter Reformation: Religion and Society in*

Early Modern Europe. New York: Cambridge University Press, 1995.

Klein, Herbert S. *The Atlantic Slave Trade.* New York: Cambridge University Press, 1999.

Kuhn, Thomas S. *The Copernican Revolution.* New York: MJF Books, 1997.

Lane, Kris. *Pillaging the Empire: Piracy in the Americas, 1500–1750.* Armok, NY: M. E. Sharpe, 1998.

Lindberg, Carter (ed.). *The European Reformation Sourcebook.* Malden, Mass.: Blackwell Publishers, 1999.

MacCulloch, Diarmaid. *The Reformation: A History.* New York: Viking Press, 2004.

Marius, R. *Martin Luther: The Christian between God and Death.* Cambridge, Mass.: Belknap Press, 1999.

McGrath, A. E. *Reformation Thought.* Third edition, Malden, Mass.: Blackwell Publishers, 1999.

Oakley, S. P. *War and Peace in the Baltic 1560–1790.* New York: Routledge, 1992.

Porter, Roy. *The Greatest Benefit to Mankind: Medical History of Humanity.* New York: W. W. Norton, 1998.

Rawlings, Helen. *The Spanish Inquisition.* Malden, Mass.: Blackwell Publishers, 2005.

Renaissance. Danbury, Connecticut: Grolier, 2002.

Roth, Mitchel P. *Crime and Punishment: A History of the Criminal Justice System.* Belmont, CA: Thomson Wadsworth, 2005.

Russell-Wood, A. J. R. *The Portuguese Empire, 1415–1808: A World on the Move.* Baltimore, MD: Johns Hopkins University Press, 1998.

Schama, Simon. *The Embarrassment of Riches: Dutch Culture in the Golden Age.* New York: Vintage Books, 1997.

Stoyle, John. *Europe Unfolding 1648–1688.* Second edition, Malden, Mass.: Blackwell Publishers, 2000.

Taylor, Alan. *American Colonies: The Settlement of North America to 1800.* New York: Penguin Books, 2003.

Tracy, J. D. *Europe's Reformations 1450–1650.* Lanham: Rowman & Littlefield, 1999.

Walvin, James. *The Quakers: Money and Morals.* London: John Murray, 1997.

Ware, Timothy. *The Orthodox Church.* New York: Penguin Books, 2004.

Wilson, P. H. *The Holy Roman Empire, 1495–1806.* New York: St. Martin's Press, 1999.

WEBSITES

BBC Online: History
www.bbc.co.uk/history

British Civil Wars, Commonwealth, and Protectorate 1638–1660
www.british-civil-wars.co.uk

Catholic Encyclopedia
www.newadvent.org/cathen/

Database of Reformation Artists
www.artcyclopedia.com/index.html

History of Protestantism
www.doctrine.org/history/

The Library of Economics and Liberty
www.econlib.org

National Gallery of Art
www.nga.gov

National Maritime Museum, Greenwich
www.nmm.ac.uk

Reformation History
www.historychannel.com

SET INDEX

PICTURE CREDITS